RECIPES FOR REFUGE

CULINARY JOURNEYS TO AMERICA

REFUGEE WOMEN'S ALLIANCE

ReWA students, staff, and supporters provided all the recipes in our cookbook. A generous team of volunteers tested the recipes and adapted them to appeal to a wide range of palates. In some cases, they adjusted proportions, ingredients, and spices to benefit our diverse cookbook readers. Occasionally, a traditional ingredient was so hard to find in Western markets that our team elected to suggest a good substitute.

Empowering families • Strengthening communities

Published by Refugee Women's Alliance, Seattle
rewa.org

Edited and designed by Girl Friday Productions
girlfridayproductions.com

Design: Paul Barrett
Editorial: Leslie Miller, Kristin Mehus-Roe, Tiffany Taing, Karen Upson, Keerthi Sudevan, Lois Baron, Connie Binder
Image credits: cover and interior food photos: Hilary McMullen with Jenna Andersen Creative; interior portraits: Manuela Insixiengmay
Photo team: Jill Raynor-Holdcroft (producer), Jean Galton (stylist), Heather Hollenbeck (styling assistant), Sunny Giron (styling assistant), Beth Batson (props and sets), Jessica Yager (photo assistant)

ISBN (hardcover): 978-0-578-57359-5
ISBN (paperback): 978-0-578-57358-8

First edition

CONTENTS

Come, Sit, Eat . . .
STARTERS, SIDES, AND SNACKS

Community Feasts and Flavors
MAIN DISHES AND HEARTY SOUPS

A Taste of Home

DESSERTS AND DRINKS

INTRODUCTION

By Refugee Women's Alliance Executive Director Mahnaz K. Eshetu

"Women are not only inherently valuable as individuals, but they are also the cornerstones of healthy and stable communities."
—Mahnaz K. Eshetu

I was about ten years old, in my home country of Iran, and my family had invited a few friends over for dinner. My father had just returned from his annual hunting trip and brought home pheasant. It was prepared as pomegranate *khoresh*; all day the scent of the pheasant cooking on the stove teased me, and I could hardly wait for dinner to be served. In my impatience, I chatted incessantly while jumping around and repeatedly checking in on the progress of the main dish.

As the time drew near, I begged my parents to let me be the one to present the festive entrée to our guests. When the khoresh was ready to be served, my mother agreed to allow me to carry it to the dining table from the kitchen. I pushed my way through the door into our dining room, and I grinned at our guests with pride. Seconds later, I stumbled and lost my grasp on the serving dish. I froze as the khoresh crashed to the ground, splattering in all directions. I will never forget the looks on my parents' faces—surely mirroring the horror and disbelief on my own.

From then on, my reputation in the family was sealed: I was the clumsy one who could not be trusted in the kitchen. Is it any wonder that I later went on to a career in finance?

Thankfully, I am still thrilled by the preparations and the excitement around having guests over for dinner. And I still make pomegranate khoresh for special occasions, even though the memory of that day returns every time I carry that dish from the kitchen to the dining room.

Mealtime around a large table, the whiff of a certain aroma, and the sight of a special ingredient: this act of eating together and of all the minute details that accompany food preparation and consumption create magical, indelible memories for people the world over. It should be no surprise then that people who live far from their childhood homes often try to re-create those treasured mealtime moments in their new homes and lives. This process can ease homesickness and temporarily minimize the weight of vast distances. It can also be a powerful way to share your culture and heritage with new friends, neighbors, and colleagues.

Our students, clients, staff, volunteers, and supporters at Refugee Women's Alliance (ReWA) have been communing together over food since our organization was founded. The working dinner, the celebratory potluck, and the baby-shower meals are as much a part of ReWA's history as the story of our growth as a wraparound social service agency. We are pleased to share part of that history with you in the pages of this cookbook.

Generous students and staff have shared their favorite recipes, and a large team of volunteers helped us produce this beautiful book. Some of the cooks in this collection have even graciously shared the unique stories of their own journeys here. Woven together, these personal histories provide a remarkable testament to the strength and resilience of the diverse members of our ReWA family. I hope *Recipes for Refuge* touches you as deeply as it has touched me.

WE ARE REFUGEE WOMEN'S ALLIANCE

The Refugee Women's Alliance is a nonprofit, multi-ethnic organization that promotes inclusion, independence, personal leadership, and strong communities by providing refugee and immigrant women and their families with culturally and linguistically appropriate services. ReWA advocates for social justice, public policy changes, and equal access to services while respecting cultural values and the right to self-determination.

Where did it all begin? In 1985, a group of refugee women—who were still in the process of settling into this newly adopted country—saw a great need among other refugee and low-income immigrant women. They got together on their coffee breaks and during meals after working at their new jobs to discuss how they could make the process of transition into this new society easier for their friends. Through their own difficult experiences, they saw ways to make things easier for other women. They were determined to create a safe space to offer services that met particular needs of female refugees.

After much discussion and debate, they came up with a structure for a new kind of agency where refugee and immigrant women would offer services in their native languages to other women in similar situations. They had seen how this could work well when they were still living in refugee camps. All the same, their decision to staff the new organization's programs with former refugee and immigrant women—whenever possible—was highly unusual at the time; it was a model that didn't exist in Seattle. This would not be a place where the leaders and role models were Americans. Instead, they recognized the strength and power of a model where the majority of a student's teachers and advocates were members of her own community. While helping women who sought their services, they would also help empower their female staff members. They would create jobs that filled a critical and unmet need, and they did so with great cultural sensitivity and respect for each and every individual involved in the new organization.

How could they make it possible, though, for the many mothers with young children to participate? The solution they came up with was brilliant in its simplicity. They would couple the classes, workshops, and services for the adult women with high-quality childcare and age-appropriate educational programs for the participants' children. ReWA's founding mothers recognized that when a mother knows her children are secure and supported, it frees her up to focus on her own personal growth and development.

When the new organization opened its doors to refugee and immigrant women, its staff offered English classes, support for accessing services from government social service agencies, assistance to domestic violence survivors, and childcare.

As ReWA's founding mothers were all Southeast Asian women, they originally named the organization the South East Asian Women's Alliance (SEAWA). By 1992, refugees from other parts of the world were already showing up for the organization's English classes. That year the board of directors elected to change the name of the organization to Refugee Women's Alliance. Whether the refugee was from Vietnam, Ethiopia, or Ukraine, the overarching need was the same.

Today, ReWA serves low-income women, men, and children of all ages who reside in Seattle and the greater Puget Sound region. All of ReWA's services are rooted in the philosophy of respect and empowerment. We help our students and clients leverage their own strengths by providing them with additional knowledge, skills, and support. Our ultimate goal is to make it possible for participating families to achieve self-sufficiency and independence. ReWA's 145 staff members serve over 12,000 refugees and immigrants each year at ten different site locations and provide ongoing support to over 4,000 clients. ReWA's current client composition is the following: 39 percent from Asia, 38 percent from Africa, 9 percent from the Middle East, and 5 percent from Latin America. Additionally, 64 percent of our clients identify as female, and 36 percent identify as male.

Today, we are proud of the ten core programs we operate throughout King County, including Seattle:

- **Family Empowerment:** case management support helps families achieve self-sufficiency and includes interpretation services, referrals, workshops, and application assistance. Services to 751 individuals and families in 2017.
- **English as a Second Language Classes:** ESL classes to improve English language skills. Two hundred sixty-four adult English language students in 2017.
- **Employment and Vocational Training:** job-readiness training, job search/placement support, and job-retention services. Seven hundred forty-nine participants in 2017.
- **Youth Program:** low-income refugee and immigrant students (first grade through young adult) receive out-of-school support. Served 347 youth in 2017.
- **Housing and Homelessness Prevention:** emergency help for clients who are homeless or at risk of homelessness. Ninety-six percent of those served through our Rapid Rehousing Project in 2017 maintained housing for at least six months.

- **Licensed Behavioral Health:** mental health counseling, consultation, support groups, and case management in clients' native languages. Supported 238 patients on average each month in 2017.
- **Naturalization and Legal Services:** citizenship classes, green card/naturalization application assistance, advocacy at immigration interviews, and free legal clinics. Approximately four hundred ReWA clients submit naturalization or green card applications annually.
- **Senior Program:** social networking opportunities with other neighborhood residents to reduce isolation and promote emotional health and well-being.
- **Early Learning Center (ELC):** licensed and accredited high-quality, multi-language preschool and childcare. One hundred thirty families received early childhood education support and parenting workshops in 2017 from two locations. (And from three locations in 2018!)
- **Domestic Violence and Human Trafficking:** legal assistance, community outreach, support groups, and case management services. Seven hundred fifty-two individual clients received support in 2017.

This is the only Seattle-area nonprofit organization that provides services to such a wide range of refugees and immigrants from over seventy different home countries. Additionally, this agency likely has the most diversity in both client and staff populations. Over 85 percent of our staff are refugees or immigrants, and, collectively, our staff members speak over fifty different languages and dialects. ReWA has deep respect for the languages and cultures of participants and an unparalleled level of cultural competence.

ReWA's board of directors is composed of leaders within their fields and includes lawyers, finance professionals, professors, engineers, and other inspiring members of the community. In addition to our volunteer board, ReWA also benefits from the support of a community of bridge builders and hundreds of program and classroom volunteers who do everything from teaching English to adults to mentoring the students in our Youth Program.

Because of this strong community support and the expertise of our staff, ReWA is one of the few local organizations that is able to serve all groups of people who have recently arrived in this country. We are particularly proud of maintaining a nimble approach to meeting the needs of the changing refugee populations that arrive in our region.

THE MAKING OF *RECIPES FOR REFUGE*

Sharing meals is as much a part of ReWA as providing English classes and wraparound support services and programs. ReWA's founding mothers met over lunches and dinners as they developed its organizational structure and board bylaws. As far back as we can remember, staff members have brought dishes to share with each other during regular workdays and for more organized staff potlucks and parties. We mark everything from holidays to agency milestones by communing together over food. ReWA students also celebrate their achievements and class graduations with potluck parties. It is no surprise then that ReWA staff members have talked for years about creating a cookbook of our diverse recipes to share with supporters and the wider public. The challenges of publishing a book always prevented that idea from coming to fruition.

Then, in late 2018, Leslie "LAM" Miller, cofounder of Girl Friday Productions, attended a ReWA Cooking Party & Dinner. That day, she learned how to make Somali rice, *bariis*; ate a delicious meal of Somali food; and heard that ReWA students and clients represent over seventy countries from around the world. A lightbulb went on. In addition to owning a book production company, LAM had written and produced cookbooks in the past. For her, it was obvious that ReWA should make a cookbook and present the rich recipes and cultures of ReWA's family to the world. She talked with ReWA Bridge Builder volunteer Betina Simmons Blaine, and the idea of a cookbook was born.

Girl Friday Productions generously agreed to donate all of their book production services to this project—from editing to design to print brokering. Additionally, they helped connect ReWA to copyeditor Keerthi Sudevan, proofreader Lois Baron, and indexer Connie Binder, who all agreed to donate their time to making our cookbook.

Betina Simmons Blaine and ReWA staffer Ramlah Ringold Olt spent tireless hours collecting recipes and the incredible and often harrowing journey stories from ReWA staff and clients, testing and retesting aforementioned recipes, and managing projects.

Betina also recruited photography producer Jill Raynor-Holdcroft to the volunteer cookbook team. Jill put together a group of portrait and food photographers and stylists, including Hilary McMullen, Manuela Insixiengmay, Jenna Andersen, and Sunny Giron, who volunteered to capture the stunning images you see within these pages.

Finally, many volunteers participated in the process of collecting family recipes and journey stories including Stephanie Mano, Kris Morada, Idil Danaan, Rahima Houssein, Sunny Giron, Jennifer Clancy, Rachel Werther, and Heather Hollenbeck. Additional help came from Glazer's Camera owners Rebecca Kaplan and Ari Lackman, Jenna Andersen Creative, Kezira Café owner Nigist Kidane, Xalwo Kismayo, Sharon Mentyka, and Rainier Beach Urban Farm. ReWA executive director Mahnaz Kourourian Eshetu and staff Karin Kaups, Lisa McCormick, Emily Nielson, Emily Ausema, and Yuliya Matyushkina also helped produce this book. The collection that resulted is stunning in its scope and breathtaking in its diversity. Just like ReWA. We are proud to share this snapshot of our organization with you.

Best of all, the proceeds from ReWA's *Recipes for Refuge* will go toward creating a safer space in Seattle for local refugee and immigrant families. The thousands of students and clients who seek services and participate in programs at ReWA benefit annually, as do the hundreds of staff members who work for ReWA across our different locations throughout the greater Puget Sound region. Our community partners benefit, too, since ReWA collaborates directly with them on tackling thorny issues of the day, such as homelessness and social inequality. Our diverse neighbors also benefit when they join us for joyful community celebrations like our annual International Women's Day party. Win, win, win.

Come, Sit, Eat . . .

STARTERS, SIDES, AND SNACKS

MAIMUN

ReWA Supporter • Malaysia

Maimun was always a very good student. As a young girl in Malaysia, she dreamed of becoming a teacher. However, as the eldest child in a very large family, whose mother died in childbirth when Maimun was only thirteen years old, she could not follow that path in her home country. A few years after losing her mother, Maimun felt compelled to drop out of high school, find a job, and help support her seven younger siblings.

After working for several years, she found a position as a typist in the administrative department of a college where some of her colleagues were US Peace Corps workers. She met and fell in love with one of the Americans there. They married in 1970 and he brought her home with him. She has lived in the Seattle area ever since.

Once her two children were old enough, Maimun returned to school at a community college, where she earned first her GED and then her associate's degree. She then transferred to the University of Washington, where she went on to earn a BS in materials science engineering. Maimun enjoyed a successful career as a Boeing engineer until she retired in 2014, soon after watching the successful first flight of the Dreamliner—her final project.

She has always been a fabulous cook and loves to host parties. Her nephew, Peter Ringold, enjoyed eating her food so much that he asked her to teach him her Malaysian recipes. Peter is now a chef at Cozymeal, where he continues to prepare Southeast Asian dishes. Maimun considers it an honor that Peter shares her recipes with so many diverse people.

Chicken Satay

Provided by Peter Ringold in collaboration with his aunt, Maimun Hassan Ringold. Peter is a chef at Cozymeal.

Chicken satay is a staple of Malaysian street food. Traditionally, each open-air food market has a satay stand. As cooks grill row upon row of marinated meat on bamboo sticks, they tend the fire with long, wide fans. The passersby cannot help but be drawn to the savory aroma and mesmerizing scene.

INGREDIENTS

4 lemongrass stalks, white part
    only, chopped then pureed
¼ cup shallots, minced
2 tablespoons ground coriander
2 tablespoons ground cumin
1 teaspoon ground turmeric

2 teaspoons minced garlic
1½ teaspoons kosher salt
½ cup canola oil
1 cup palm sugar
3 pounds boneless chicken thighs,
    cut into 1-inch pieces

The night before you plan to cook, soak bamboo skewers in water to prevent burning while cooking. While they soak, prepare and marinate the chicken.

1. In a wide bowl, whisk together all marinade ingredients.
2. Add chicken pieces to bowl and mix until all chicken is evenly coated.
3. Transfer marinated chicken to a glass dish with cover. Seal and marinate overnight in refrigerator.
4. The next day, drain bamboo skewers.
5. Skewer five chicken pieces per stick. The pieces should not be pressed together.
6. Wrap exposed end of each skewer with tinfoil to prevent burning.
7. Grill over direct heat until the chicken pieces are cooked through, turning frequently.

Tip: Channel your inner Malaysian grill master and use a handheld fan to tend to your skewers as they cook!

Ceviche

Provided by Rebecca Escamilla, ReWA Childcare Lead Teacher, Pre-3 Classroom

A ReWA childcare lead teacher, Rebecca "Becky" Escamilla, was born in the US, but her parents moved here as immigrants from Mexico in the early 1970s. She has five siblings and two children.

Becky likes to make crab-and-shrimp ceviche when she gets together with her large extended family or friends. Across Mexico, you will find various takes on the classic ceviche, including different combinations of fresh fish and shellfish. The classic way to make ceviche is to begin with raw shrimp, as Becky does. By marinating the shrimp in fresh lemon juice—until the shrimp turn pink—you essentially cook them in acid before they ever meet the other ingredients.

INGREDIENTS

8–10 lemons, juiced or about 1½ cups (enough to marinate shrimp)

1½ pounds raw shrimp or prawns, peeled and deveined

1 pound cooked, picked crab meat

1 bunch of cilantro, leaves only, chopped

1 red onion, peeled and diced

2 cucumbers, peeled and diced

5 tomatoes, chopped

4 avocados, peeled, pitted, and chopped

4 serrano chilis, chopped (remove seeds for a milder flavor)

½ cup Clamato juice (store-bought or homemade, recipe follows)

Salt

Tostadas or tortilla chips for dipping

1. Pour the lemon juice into a large bowl. Add shrimp to it, and toss to coat. Cover and refrigerate for 1 hour, or until the shrimp turn pink.
2. Add remaining ingredients to the bowl and stir to combine. Enjoy with tostadas or tortilla chips as an appetizer or your main course.

Yield: 7 cups

Homemade Clamato

Provided by Betina Simmons Blaine, ReWA Bridge Builder Volunteer

Becky, a busy working mom, usually uses the pre-prepared Clamato in her ceviche. If you prefer to make your own, here is our recipe, equally delicious in ceviche as it is added to a glass of cold beer to make a *michelada*.

INGREDIENTS

46 ounces tomato juice

10 ounces bottled clam juice

¼ cup fresh lemon juice

1 teaspoon Worcestershire sauce

¼ teaspoon hot sauce

½ teaspoon salt or celery salt

½ teaspoon red chili pepper flakes

Sugar

1. Mix all ingredients together in a jar or a container with a lid.
2. Seal, shake, and taste for sugar. Keep refrigerated.

Curry Puffs

Provided by Peter Ringold, ReWA Supporter

Peter Ringold grew up eating his aunt's Malaysian foods. After returning from a back-packing trip through Southeast Asia—where he spent significant time with his Malaysian relatives—Chef Peter began his formal foray into the culinary world. He opened a Malaysian-inspired street food restaurant and is now a chef at Cozymeal. Chef Peter's successes have been featured in the *Seattle Times, Seattle Met*, the *Stranger*, and on the Food Network.

INGREDIENTS

Filling
¼ cup canola oil
½ cup diced red onions
1 tablespoon curry powder
   (Baba's brand if possible)
1 teaspoon chili powder
¼ teaspoon chili paste (such
   as *sambal oelek*)
½ teaspoon ground turmeric
1 tablespoon sugar
1 teaspoon salt

¼ teaspoon black pepper
¼ cup diced carrots
¼ cup peas
1 cup diced boiled potatoes

Dough
¼ cup water
¼ cup canola oil
½ teaspoon salt
1 cup all-purpose flour
Canola oil for frying

Filling

1. Heat ¼ cup canola oil in a sauté pan over medium heat. Add diced onions and fry until golden.
2. In small bowl, mix curry powder, chili powder, chili paste, turmeric, sugar, salt, and pepper to make a paste. Add to onions in the pan. Reduce heat to medium-low and fry until aromatic.

3. Add carrots and peas. Fry for 5 more minutes and remove from the heat.
4. Place diced potato in a large bowl. Add the onion mixture to it and combine. Set aside.

Dough

1. To make the dough, mix water, oil, and salt together in a large bowl.
2. Add flour and mix by hand until a sticky dough forms. Cover with a cloth and let it rest for 30 minutes.
3. When ready to assemble, pull off golf-ball-sized portions of dough. With each ball, first roll between your palms to create a smooth sphere, then place on a floured surface and flatten into a circle with a rolling pin.

Puffs

1. Add about 2 tablespoons of filling to half of each dough circle.
2. Fold dough in half to create semicircle. Pinch together edges of dough and twist to seal, creating a crimped edge. Repeat with remaining puffs.
3. Pour canola oil to a depth of 1 inch in a heavy pan on a stove and heat over medium. When the oil is hot, add puffs in batches. Fry for about 2 minutes per side, or until golden brown. Keep curry puffs slightly separated while frying.
4. Remove from the heat and allow them to cool in a colander or on a cooling rack before transferring to a platter lined with paper towel.

HODAN

SeaTac ESL Student • Somalia

Hodan is from Marka, Somalia. Her family fled the Somali Civil War for Ethiopia when she was about four years old. She arrived in the US in 2008, first in Maine, then went from there to Arizona with her family before moving to Seattle on her own. She got married three years ago, and now works as a home health aide, as well as part-time for Amazon scanning packages. She wishes she had the opportunity to go to school earlier in her life, but she is happy now that she is able to attend ESL classes with ReWA, which she began in late 2018. She likes Seattle for its beauty and abundant job opportunities.

AMINA

SeaTac ESL Student • Somalia

Amina is from Kismayo, Somalia. There, her family farmed many crops: sweet potatoes, melons, potatoes, peppers, sorghum, maize, tomatoes, green beans, ginger, mango, and coconut. Before she was married, she also used to catch shrimp and fish.

The lawlessness and chaos of the civil war took a toll on Amina's family; her father was shot and killed during a robbery, and then her mother fell and died three days later because there was no hospital to go to. Amina does not know what happened to her two brothers. Like many Somali people, Amina fled the war with her husband and children in 1992. They lived in three different refugee camps in Kenya, where there were as many as 450,000 Somalis by 2012. The family grew from two to seven children during the 18 years they lived in the Kenyan camps.

Amina and some of her family joined her son in Seattle in 2015. She still has family in Kenya, and she misses them very much. She particularly misses her daughter, whom she is always worried about but whom she carries with her in her heart. She is grateful that there is no war here and that we are free and safe and have functioning schools and hospitals.

Amina enjoys the ESL classes she has been taking for two years through ReWA, cooking, her family, and being with her grandchildren. She likes to spend time with her ten-year-old son, and is teaching him to make bread. When he was recently hospitalized, she felt so fortunate that he could get the care he needed here. To Amina, "Freedom is everything."

Yield: About 30

Sambusa

Provided by Amina, Hodan, and Sahra, ReWA Students

These savory fried pastries are often served with tea in Somalia (*asariye*), as an appetizer, or as part of any festive meal in both Somalia and Ethiopia. Both Amina and Hodan were taught to make these as children. They can be made with beef, lamb, chicken, or fish, though beef is used in this recipe. Hodan keeps hers simple with just beef, onions, chilis, and garlic, and she fries them in olive oil. Amina prefers to include a variety of vegetables. Flavorings can also be customized, but sambusa are traditionally a bit spicy and aromatic.

Sahra's mother taught her this recipe, and she makes it for Ramadan to break the fast as well as for other evening gatherings and celebrations. She usually makes 30 sambusa at a time, but on occasion makes up to 400.

INGREDIENTS

Filling
2 tablespoons vegetable oil
½–1 tablespoon xawaash (recipe follows)
1 red onion, finely chopped
1 carrot, finely chopped
1 bell pepper, finely chopped (optional)
1 russet potato, peeled and
    finely cubed (optional)
1 clove garlic, finely chopped (optional)
2 pounds lean ground beef
½ cup fresh cilantro, finely chopped
1 chili pepper (jalapeño or serrano
    work well), finely chopped
2 teaspoons salt
½ teaspoon ground black pepper

Pastry
3 cups flour
2 tablespoons vegetable oil
¼ teaspoon salt
1 cup lukewarm water
Oil for deep frying

Filling

1. Heat oil in a large skillet over medium heat. Add xawaash and sauté for 1 minute. Add onion and carrot. If you are using bell pepper, potato, and garlic, add those as well. Sauté until onion is translucent.
2. Add ground beef and stir often until brown.
3. Add cilantro, chili pepper, salt, and pepper, and sauté for another minute.
4. Remove from the heat and set aside to cool while you make the pastry.

Pastry

1. Mix the flour, oil, and salt in a bowl. Slowly add water while mixing with a fork.
2. Once the dough is ready, turn it out onto a floured surface and knead for 5–10 minutes or until smooth and pliable.
3. Form the dough into a ball, lightly coat it with oil, and place it in a clean bowl. Leave to rest for 15 minutes.
4. When dough is rested and filling is cool, briefly knead dough again, then divide into 8 equal balls.
5. Using a rolling pin, roll each ball flat, about the size of a dinner plate. Cut each into quarters.
6. Form each quarter into a cone by folding the sides and pinching them together. It should resemble an ice cream cone.
7. Fill each cone with some of the meat and vegetable mixture.
8. Tuck the pointed top down over the sealed edges and pinch. Use water to seal as needed. Repeat with the remaining quarters.
9. To cook, heat several inches of oil over medium heat in a heavy pan. Test if the oil is hot enough by slipping a small piece of dough into the oil—if it floats immediately to the surface, the oil is ready to use.
10. Fry several sambusa at a time until the dough turns golden brown on all sides.
11. Drain on paper towels and serve warm.

Yield: About 1½ cups

Xawaash

Provided by Betina Simmons Blaine, ReWA Bridge Builder Volunteer

Translated from Arabic, *xawaash* means "essential," and that's what this spice mix is to every Somali cook. There are many regional variations, so feel free to alter proportions to suit your palate.

INGREDIENTS

½ cup cumin seeds

½ cup coriander seeds

2 tablespoon black peppercorns

2 tablespoons fenugreek seeds

1 cinnamon stick

1 tablespoon green cardamom pods

1 teaspoon whole cloves

1 tablespoon ground ginger

1 teaspoon freshly ground nutmeg

2 tablespoons turmeric powder

1. Warm a skillet over medium heat.
2. Add all spices except ginger, nutmeg, and turmeric, and toast for 4–5 minutes, stirring frequently and taking care not to let the spices burn.
3. Remove from heat and allow to cool.
4. Transfer toasted spices to a spice grinder, or into a mortar. Process or grind with a pestle until fine.
5. Transfer to an airtight container and stir in turmeric, ginger, and nutmeg.

Beet Salad Vinaigrette

Ukrainian version provided by Mira Manusova, former ReWA Finance Director. Russian version provided by Yuliya Matyushkina, ReWA ESL Coordinator.

This salad is good for parties because you can make it a day in advance, and according to Mira, a Ukrainian, it tastes even better the next day, making it her favorite dish to bring to ReWA potlucks. According to Russian Yuliya, every Eastern European cook and homemaker knows how to make a version of this beloved salad. Her version adds sauerkraut.

INGREDIENTS

3 medium beets, scrubbed

3 medium potatoes, scrubbed

3 medium carrots, scrubbed

3–4 medium pickles

2 tablespoons olive oil, divided

1½ teaspoons white vinegar

1 small onion, finely chopped
  (about ½ cup)

½ cup sauerkraut, drained (optional)

1. In a medium pot, boil beets for 1 hour or until they can be pierced easily with a knife.
2. In a separate pot, boil potatoes and carrots for about 30 minutes, or until a knife goes smoothly through the potatoes. Do not overcook the potatoes.
3. Drain the vegetables and refrigerate to cool quickly.
4. Peel the skins from the potatoes and carrots. Dice pickles, potatoes, carrots. Mix these vegetables together in one bowl with onion.
5. Separately, peel and dice beets. Mix beets with 1 tablespoon oil to limit the beet's color spreading to the other ingredients.
6. Add beets to other ingredients. Add vinegar and the remaining tablespoon of oil. Mix gently. Add sauerkraut, if using.
7. Refrigerate until ready to serve.

OKSANA

ReWA Immigration Attorney • Ukraine

Oksana Bilobran was born and raised in Ukraine. After receiving her first law degree, she met her future husband, Brian Bennett, an American attorney, while they were both legal interns at the Public Interest Environmental Law Organization in Lviv, Ukraine. This posed an 8,000-mile dilemma for the young couple. Following her heart, Oksana moved to the US in 2004. After graduating from the University of Washington Law School, she started practicing Immigration Law in 2007. Oksana became the First Lady of the City of Burien in 2012 when Brian became mayor of the city, a position he held for a two-year term. Oksana and Brian have three young children.

In 2016, Oksana became ReWA's staff Immigration Attorney. At ReWA, she oversees the legal immigration program, which includes assisting people with the US naturalization process and the adjustment of naturalization status for refugees and their family members based on new arrivals and other changes in their circumstances.

Oksana has been instrumental in helping ReWA respond to the rapid changes in national immigration law that have taken place since 2016. She has played a valuable leadership role in our community with the wide scope of legal work she has undertaken, including organizing Know Your Rights workshops, facilitating immigration law clinics, and meeting with migrants seeking asylum being held at the detention center in SeaTac, Washington.

Vegetarian Borsch

Provided by Oksana Bilobran, ReWA Immigration Attorney

Borsch is the soul of Ukrainian food, and it has been perfected, modified, and passed on for generations. Oksana says, "In our house, cooking borsch is how we show love for our family. When we travel, we are always excited to eat authentic food in new locations. We love sushi, pizza, and tacos. A few days into a trip, though, my kids usually start talking about borsch. They know that every time we return home, my mom will greet us with a hot pot of fresh homemade borsch. The taste of it reassures my kids that Grandma loves us, and missed us when we were away, and that she is ready to hear about all our adventures as we nourish our bodies with its bright red goodness."

INGREDIENTS

4 tablespoons olive oil
3 medium beets, peeled and grated
2 carrots, peeled and grated
1 medium onion, finely diced
2 tablespoons white vinegar
1 teaspoon sugar
3 tablespoons tomato sauce
8 cups water

3 medium potatoes, peeled
   and cut into large dice
½ head of small cabbage, shredded
2 bay leaves
Salt and pepper
3 tablespoons chopped dill and/or parsley
2 large garlic cloves, pressed or minced
Sour cream, for garnish

1. Heat olive oil in a large heavy-bottomed skillet. Add beets, carrots, and diced onion and sauté for 5 minutes or until limp. Add white vinegar, sugar, and tomato sauce. Mix thoroughly and sauté until they soften, stirring occasionally for about 10 minutes. Remove from the heat and set aside.
2. Heat 8 cups water in large soup pot. Add potatoes and let them cook for about 10 minutes.
3. Add shredded cabbage and the sautéed beets, carrots, and onion mixture. Cook for another 10 minutes or until potatoes can be easily pierced with a knife.

4. Add bay leaves, pepper, salt, chopped parsley or dill, and pressed garlic. Stir and immediately cover, removing from heat. Cover pot for 20 minutes to let the flavors meld.

5. Serve in individual bowls, topped with a dollop of sour cream.

Jiaozi

Provided by Annie Liu, Accounts Payable Specialist

Jiaozi, or dumplings, are a treat from Northern China and are traditionally served on special occasions, like Chinese New Year. On that occasion, families eat jiaozi when the clock strikes midnight. For people whose living conditions have improved, making and enjoying jiaozi has become more common. This is certainly the case for Annie. When she grew up in the small farming community of Heilongjiang Province, her family had very little money, and jiaozi. Jiaozi were a special treat for her as a child. Now, though, Annie is the accounts payable specialist at ReWA and has both the means and the time to make jiaozi more frequently. If you are pressed for time, you can purchase wonton wrappers to substitute for the dough.

While you can eat jiaozi on their own, they taste even better with the dipping sauce.

INGREDIENTS

Dough
¾–1 cup cold water
2 cups all-purpose flour, plus
    extra for dusting

Filling
1 tablespoon vegetable oil
3 small fried tofu cakes, chopped
    to the size of grains of rice
2 cups fresh shiitake mushrooms,
    chopped to the size of grains of rice
½ teaspoon ginger, minced
1 pinch ground Szechuan pepper powder
1 pinch ground anise powder
3 tablespoons soy sauce

1 teaspoon salt, plus more as needed
½ napa cabbage, sliced thinly
1 small bunch of fresh dill, chopped

Dipping Sauce
½ cup soy sauce
1 teaspoon seasoned rice wine vinegar
½ teaspoon sesame oil
Optional additions: red pepper flakes,
    minced garlic, fermented tofu, chive
    flowers, or any spice you like

Dough

1. Add up to ¾ cup of very cold water into the flour while continuously stirring. Knead the dough, adding more water if needed, to make it nice and pliable.
2. Cover with a clean dish towel and set aside. (Annie says her mother used to cover the dough with a dish towel, but she was very particular about it being freshly washed and, thus, extra clean.)

Filling

1. Heat oil on medium in a wok. Add tofu and mushrooms, and mix for 1 minute. Add the ginger, Szechuan pepper powder, anise powder, soy sauce, and salt. Mix until cooked through. Set aside.
2. Sprinkle a little salt over the cabbage slices. Wait 2 minutes, then layer the slices between two sheets of paper towels and gently press out excess water.
3. Add the cabbage and dill into the cooked mixture. Add more salt as needed.

Assembly

1. Dust a cutting board with flour. Roll the dough into a rope about 1½ inches in diameter. Cut the rope of dough into small ½-inch coin-shaped pieces. Use a rolling pin to shape the small pieces of dough into thin circles, about 3½ inches in diameter. Dust the rolling pin and circles of dough with more flour to prevent sticking.
2. Place 1 tablespoon of filling in the center of each thin circle of dough. Fold each into a semicircle, press the edges together, and give the dumpling a little twist to seal the dough tightly and prevent the filling from leaking.
3. If boiling, bring a pot of water to a boil. Add several dumplings at once. Stir gently to prevent them from sticking to one another. Once the dumplings fill with air and puff up like balloons, use a slotted spoon to take them out and place them in colander to drain. Once drained, transfer the dumplings to a dish lined with aluminum foil.
4. If steaming, place the dumplings on a well-oiled surface in a steamer basket over boiling water. Steam for approximately 6 minutes, or until done.

Dipping Sauce

1. Mix the ingredients together in a bowl. Add any optional ingredients as preferred.

THOA

Chef and Owner of Chinoise Sushi Bar & Asian Grill and Sushi Chinoise • Vietnam

Thoa was born in Saigon, Vietnam, and was eleven years old when her city fell to communist control. She will never forget the terrible chaos of that journey out of the country. She saw sugar cane fields set on fire, panic in the streets, and confusion in the dark aboard the deck of a Navy ship packed tightly with jostling people.

Her family spent time in a refugee camp in Guam, and then a second camp in Pennsylvania, before they made their way to Colorado. They settled just outside of Denver. As the eldest of five children, she grew up cooking for her family and loved being in the kitchen. Thoa recalls, "My parents always bought chicken. I got really good at cooking chicken. Chicken curry, roasted chicken, sweet-and-sour chicken, salted . . . steamed . . . boiled . . . fried chicken."

All those chicken dishes might have scared some people out of the kitchen for good. Thoa, though, considered chicken—and the lure of the meal—an exciting challenge. As an adult, she opened her first restaurant in 1996, the original Chinoise Café on Queen Anne Hill in Seattle. Chinoise specializes in Pan-Pacific Rim cuisine, fresh sushi delicacies, seafood, and vegetable dishes. The restaurant grew to three locations by 2000. Thoa also opened three other restaurants, The Islander in 2003, Wabi-Sabi Sushi Bar & Restaurant, and the award-winning Thoa's Restaurant & Lounge, both in 2009, and Sushi Chinoise in 2016.

Today, Thoa lives on Mercer Island, Washington, with her husband and two children.

Yield: 6 servings

Saigon Chicken, Cabbage, and Mint Salad

Provided by Thoa Nguyen, Owner of Chinoise Café and Refugee from Vietnam

Thoa Nyugen, a refugee from Vietnam, opened her first restaurant, Chinoise Café, in the Queen Anne neighborhood of Seattle in 1996. She has opened several other Asian fusion and sushi restaurants since that time, including a second Chinoise Cafe outside of the city. While the Chinoise Cafe in Queen Anne closed in 2014, the Issaquah location remains a popular destination for local foodies.

The mint in this salad gives it a distinct fresh Southeast Asian flavor. Don't omit it!

INGREDIENTS

1 pound boneless, skinless chicken breasts
2 teaspoons salt, divided
2 tablespoons sesame oil, divided
4 cups water, or more as needed
1 inch ginger, peeled and sliced
½ jalapeño, seeds and ribs removed, sliced
2 tablespoons white wine vinegar
2 tablespoons Asian fish sauce (nam pla)

1½ tablespoons lime juice
6 cups finely shredded green cabbage (about ½ large head)
1 mango, peeled, pitted, and julienned
1 large carrot, grated
3 large radishes, grated
4 green onions, chopped
½ cup mint, chopped, divided

1. Rub chicken breasts with 1 teaspoon salt and 1 tablespoon sesame oil. Combine water, ginger, and jalapeño in a deep pot and bring to a boil over high heat. Add the chicken breasts into the boiling water; if necessary, add more water to ensure that the chicken is fully submerged.
2. Reduce heat to medium; cover and simmer for 10 minutes. Remove from the heat.
3. Leave covered and allow chicken to sit in water until cooked through, about 10 minutes. Transfer chicken to a plate, discarding the liquid. When cool enough to handle, shred chicken using two forks.

4. In a large bowl, mix together vinegar, fish sauce, lime juice, and the remaining teaspoon of salt. Add cabbage to this mix and toss. Allow it to sit for 10 minutes or until the cabbage softens slightly.
5. Add mango, carrot, radishes, green onions, ¼ cup mint, and the remaining table-spoon of sesame oil. Toss gently to mix.
6. Arrange salad on individual plates. Top with chicken and garnish with the remaining ¼ cup mint.

Patacones con Hogao

Provided by Salomé, ReWA Supporter

Salomé is a human rights lawyer and the founder of *Mindful Feminism*, an online magazine, and *patacones*, or fried plantains, are one of Salomé's favorite Colombian dishes. "A bite of this and I'm immediately transported to my grandmother's kitchen in Medellín. They're famous all around the country, and are prepared with many toppings, ranging from cheese to guacamole. But *hogao*, a tomato-and-onion sauce, is the most common—and most delicious, if you ask me!" Enjoy them on their own as a snack, or try them as a side dish when serving white fish, like tilapia or corvina.

INGREDIENTS

Hogao Sauce
3 tablespoons olive oil
1 teaspoon minced garlic
1 large white onion, chopped
4 medium-ripe tomatoes, chopped

Patacones
2 quarts of vegetable oil
6 green plantains, peeled
    and cut into halves
3 green onions, thinly sliced

Hogao Sauce

1. Warm up a skillet on medium heat and add the olive oil. After it's warm, add the minced garlic. Cook for 1 minute and then add the chopped onion and tomatoes. Reduce heat to low.
2. Simmer for about 10 minutes, occasionally stirring to prevent sticking. If you prefer your vegetables more tender, lower the heat and simmer for a few more minutes.

Patacones

1. Heat the vegetable oil in a deep stock pot. Once the oil is about 300°F, add the plantains. Stir occasionally for about 5 minutes until cooked through.

2. Remove the plantains from the oil and transfer to a paper towel. Turn off heat under the oil.

3. Crush the plantains into a pancake form by lining a cutting board with plastic wrap, placing each plantain on the cutting board one by one, and flattening the plantain with a flat object, such as a plate or another cutting board, until it's about ¼-inch thick.

4. Reheat the vegetable oil, and return the plantains to the pot for one last fry, in batches if necessary. Stir and flip the plantains occasionally until they reach a golden-brown color.

5. Remove from the pot, and place on a paper towel to absorb any excess oil. Add the hogao topping to the patacones and season with salt. *¡Y listo!* You're done.

Yield: 8 servings

Fasolia

Provided by Nigist Kidane, Owner of Kezira Café in Seattle

Fasolia is a bright, colorful mélange of green beans studded with carrots often served as part of a more complex Eritrean meal with injera. Though you may be tempted to add the garlic and ginger with the onion, Nigist says cooking the onion first separately is the East African way.

INGREDIENTS

4 cups green beans

1 yellow onion, minced

2 tablespoons water

1¼ tablespoons canola oil

4 cloves garlic, minced

2 tablespoons grated fresh ginger

1 whole large tomato, chopped

1 large carrot, cut into angled coins

¼ cup small, sweet red and
   orange bell peppers, diced

1. Trim the ends of green beans and remove any strings. Slice in half.
2. Place a sauté pan over medium heat and add onion and water. Gently fry until just translucent, for about 3 minutes.
3. Add oil, garlic, and ginger. Sauté for 5 more minutes.
4. Add tomato, green beans, and carrot. Cook for about 10 minutes, or until the beans are tender but still green. Add sweet bell pepper during the last 2 minutes of cooking.

Yield: 4 servings

Tum Bok Hoong

Provided by Carlin Yoophum, ReWA Domestic Violence Program Director

Carlin Yoophum has always loved *tum bok hoong*, or green papaya salad, but says she didn't perfect her version until she was already living here in the US. Carlin closely watched every time one of her local Thai friends made the salad for her. "She did not know that I was getting her recipe from her. I secretly observed her technique." Then Carlin repeatedly made the dish until she got it just right.

Green papaya salad is a favorite dish in both Laos and Thailand, where it is considered a comfort food. Laotians eat it as a main dish with sticky rice and dried beef or pork on the side.

INGREDIENTS

1 clove garlic

8 or more Thai red chili peppers (fresh or dried)

1 yard-long bean (also known as snake bean or Chinese long bean), cut into 1-inch pieces

2 tablespoons dried shrimp paste, divided

8 cherry tomatoes, quartered

Juice of 1 lime

2 tablespoons fish sauce (*nam pla)*

2 tablespoons palm sugar

1 Thai green papaya, peeled (generally between 4 to 6 cups for 1 papaya)

1 carrot, peeled

¼ cup roasted peanuts, unsalted, plus additional for garnish

Whole lettuce leaves for serving

Lime wedges, for garnish

1. Use mortar and pestle to pound together garlic, chilis, yard-long bean, and 1 tablespoon dried shrimp into a paste. Transfer to a bowl.
2. Add cherry tomatoes, lime juice, fish sauce, and palm sugar.
3. Julienne the papaya and carrot into long strands using a sharp knife, grater, or mandoline. Toss together into the bowl and mix with the other ingredients.
4. Add remaining dried shrimp and ¼ cup peanuts. Mix well.
5. Arrange lettuce leaves on serving platter. Top with salad. Garnish with additional peanuts and lime wedges.

NIGIST

Owner of Kezira Café • Ethiopia

Nigist Kidane is the owner and head chef at Columbia City's own Kezira Café. An immigrant from Ethiopia of Eritrean descent, Nigist was the featured chef at ReWA's first ever Recipes for Refuge Cooking Party & Dinner. That afternoon, Nigist demonstrated to an intimate group of ReWA supporters how to make an Eritrean-style chickpea stew, a red lentil stew, and stir-fried green beans called *fasolia*. Along with her demonstrations, she also provided a full meal for the guests—the recipes of which are included in this book.

Nigist arrived in the US in 1991. She lived in Oregon and North Carolina before moving to Seattle, and has always considered herself an entrepreneur. When she lived in North Carolina, she opened her first business, a small coffee shop. After tasting her delicious food, Nigist's friends and customers urged her to open a full restaurant there. In Seattle, she has owned two different restaurants, Rose Café and Kezira Café. One of the many unique features of Kezira is its Ethiopian coffee ceremony, which customers can reserve for large groups.

Gomen

Provided by Nigist Kidane, Owner of Kezira Café in Seattle

Fantastically spiced and butter soft, these Eritrean collard greens are often served alongside fresh cheese on injera.

INGREDIENTS

2 inches ginger, peeled and sliced

½ cup canola oil

8 cloves garlic, minced

4 cups collard greens, stems
   removed, chopped

½ teaspoon black pepper

1 tablespoon cardamom

½ jalapeño, sliced

1. Bring 2 cups water to a boil and add sliced ginger. Cut off heat and cover. Steep for at least 5 minutes or more for a stronger flavor. Drain water through colander into a bowl. Reserve ½ cup of the water and discard ginger.
2. Heat the oil in a heavy-bottomed pan on medium-low heat. Add garlic and sauté until soft.
3. Add ½ cup of ginger water to the fried garlic. Stir to combine and deglaze the pan.
4. Add collard greens and cook for 25 minutes, or until soft.
5. Add black pepper, cardamom, and jalapeño. Cook for an additional 5 minutes and serve.

Yield: 10 pieces

Injera

Provided by Saba and Maaza, ReWA Students

This soft, spongy bread is typical in Eritrea and Ethiopia where it is used as both a spoon and a plate. Naturally gluten free, it is made from a grasslike grain called teff. Slow fermentation makes this a nutritious food full of lactobacilli as well as calcium and potassium. *Injera*'s slightly sour taste pairs well with the strong and spicy flavors of African dishes. The meal is served on a large circle of injera, as though it were a plate. Start this recipe several days before you plan to serve it, as the batter needs to ferment for forty-eight hours (pictured, p. 63).

INGREDIENTS

8 ounces teff flour

½ package active dry yeast

1 pinch baking soda

2 cups warm water

½ teaspoon salt

Oil for brushing the pan

1. Put all the ingredients into a blender and mix on high for 1 minute.
2. Pour batter into a large bowl and cover with a cloth. Place in a warm spot and leave to ferment for 48 hours.
3. Heat a large nonstick pan or griddle over medium heat.
4. Lightly brush the pan or the griddle with oil. Ladle a small amount of batter onto it in a spiral pattern, tilting to cover the bottom of the pan with a thin, round pancake.
5. Cook on one side for about 90 seconds. Bubbles will form and pop on the surface.
6. Cover the pan and steam injera for 1 more minute.
7. Carefully remove from pan. Keep injera covered while you repeat.

Tip: The typical East African family will make a lot of injera at one time. To preserve injera, roll up one round at a time, then cut each in half. Wrap each ½ round individually in plastic wrap and store in a container in the freezer. When you want to use it, unwrap the plastic, put one ½ roll at a time in the microwave after covering with wax paper and microwave for 30 seconds. Flip over the injera, re-cover, and microwave for another 30 seconds.

Ayib

Provided by Tsege Tsegay, ReWA Youth Job Readiness Training Program Coordinator. A tribute to Mira Manusova, former ReWA Finance Director.

Tsege Tsegay arrived in the US as a refugee from Ethiopia and has been with ReWA for more than twenty-five years, since the time the organization was known as the South East Asian Women's Alliance.

It was in honor of another one of ReWA's longtime employees, Mira Manusova, that Tsege decided to share her recipe for *ayib*, homemade Ethiopian cheese. Mira came to the US as a refugee from Ukraine and worked as ReWA's finance director for over twenty-five years. Mira loves a party and excels at bringing people together. When Mira still worked at ReWA, she would ask Tsege to bring her delicious homemade Ethiopian cheese whenever there was an upcoming staff potluck (pictured, p. 63).

INGREDIENTS

½ gallon buttermilk   Salt (optional)

1. Heat buttermilk over low heat in a heavy-bottomed pot.
2. After 20 minutes, use a fork to gently lift a bit of the mixture up to see if it is forming curds. If not, turn up the heat slightly and repeat. Once solids begin forming, cook an additional 5–10 minutes or until soft cheese curds form.
3. Drain the curds (the solids) from the whey (the liquid). Discard the whey.
4. Add salt and serve alongside your favorite East African foods.

Yield: 8 servings

Olivye

Provided by Yuliya Matyushkina, ReWA ESL Coordinator

This is such a popular dish in Russia that it is also simply known as "Russian salad." Olivye can be found at most gatherings, including parties for New Year's Eve. Legend has it that this dish was invented by a Belgian cook at Hermitage, one of Moscow's most famous restaurants, and that the closely guarded recipe was stolen by a sous chef. Some of the original luxury ingredients such as grouse, veal tongue, caviar, and crayfish, changed over time to accommodate average people with more modest means.

INGREDIENTS

3 medium potatoes

4 medium carrots

1 pound of cooked chicken or ham

5 dill pickles, drained

5 hardboiled eggs, peeled

⅓ cup chopped green onion

¼ cup chopped fresh dill

1 cup mayonnaise, divided

2 cups frozen peas, thawed

1. Bring a large pot of salted water to a boil. Add potatoes and carrots, and cook for 20–30 minutes, or until they are pierced easily by a knife but are still firm.
2. Remove the vegetables. Drain and cool. When cool enough to touch, peel both potatoes and carrots.
3. Dice the chicken or ham, potatoes, carrots, pickles, and eggs into ¼-inch pieces.
4. In a medium bowl, mix together chicken or ham, potatoes, carrots, pickles, eggs, green onion, dill, and ¾ cup of mayonnaise. Add remaining mayonnaise if desired, and season with salt and pepper.
5. Fold in the peas and serve.

Sabaayad

Provided by Rahima, ReWA Volunteer

Rahima compares *sabaayad* to Indian chapati. It is also reminiscent of another Indian flatbread called paratha—crispy on the outside and tender on the inside. In Somalia, it is eaten throughout the day with any meal, as pictured, or even as a snack.

INGREDIENTS

3 cups all-purpose flour

½ teaspoon salt

3 tablespoons canola oil

1 cup warm water

½ cup oil for cooking, divided

1. In a large bowl, combine flour, salt, and 3 tablespoons oil. Slowly add warm water and knead the dough until smooth and elastic.
2. Shape the dough into a ball and brush it with a little oil. Cover and allow the dough to rest for 45 minutes to an hour.
3. Knead the dough again, and divide it into 8 balls. Roll each ball in flour.
4. Heat a skillet over medium heat. Brush with oil. When the skillet is hot, flatten a ball of dough with a rolling pin and cook until bubbles form.
5. Brush with oil and flip; repeat until it is cooked on both sides.
6. Cover the fried sabaayad to keep it warm.

Yield: 8 servings

Salvadoran Quesadilla

Provided by Alicia Guevara Molina, ReWA Youth Instructor & Post-Secondary Success Coach

Alicia Guevara Molina arrived in this country as an immigrant from El Salvador when she was only eight years old. Now on staff, she first volunteered for ReWA when she was still a college student.

In North America, we think of a tortilla with cheese when we hear the word quesadilla. In El Salvador, though, quesadilla refers to this sweet bread made with rice flour and feta cheese, which also happens to be gluten free.

Alicia says that Salvadoran quesadilla is usually eaten with coffee or hot chocolate in the afternoons or evening. It can serve as a snack, dessert or even a light dinner. For Alicia, this is a special recipe that symbolizes *abuela-nieta* (grandmother-granddaughter) bonding time, as they traditionally make this dish together. To make it, "we usually clear the kitchen table and set up our cooking station there, where we then end up with flour and cheese on our hands, and batter on my face!"

INGREDIENTS

2 cups rice flour
1 teaspoon baking powder
A pinch of salt
1 cup sugar, divided
2 cups grated or crumbled feta
   cheese, or other grated hard
   cheese such as parmesan

2 cups milk, divided
¼ cup butter at room temperature,
   plus more to grease the pan
4 eggs, yolks and whites separated
2 tablespoons sesame seeds

1. Preheat oven to 350°F.
2. Whisk together rice flour, baking powder, and salt in a large mixing bowl.
3. Add ½ cup of the feta cheese and ½ cup of the milk.
4. Mix well, then add another ½ cup of cheese and ½ cup of milk. Mix again.
5. Add ½ cup of sugar and mix.

6. Repeat steps 3–5. It improves the final texture of the bread if you add each of these ingredients a little at a time.
7. Add butter and mix.
8. Add the egg yolks only and mix well.
9. Beat egg whites in a separate bowl with a whisk or hand mixer until stiff peaks form.
10. Fold in beaten egg whites to the rest of the batter until just combined.
11. Butter a 9-inch round cake pan or 12 muffin tins.
12. Pour batter into pan or divide among tins. Spread evenly.
13. Sprinkle sesame seeds on the top.
14. Bake 15–20 minutes for muffins and 30–45 minutes for cake. Quesadilla is done when inserted toothpick comes out clean.

Yield: 4 servings, or about 12 canjeero

Canjeero

Provided by Asho, ReWA Student

Also known as *lahoh* in some regions, this Somali breakfast crepe is traditionally made with maize, wheat, or sorghum flour. There are endless variations, and every household has a favorite recipe. Asho's version is richer than most, and includes milk, egg, and the novel addition of Cream of Wheat, or farina, then fermented overnight. Although most families make their own, in many towns and villages, vendors sell *canjeero* door to door early in the morning. It is typically served with tea for breakfast, with sugar or honey and drizzled with ghee or sesame oil. Children often eat it soaked in *shaah*, or Somali tea (see recipe, p. 159). It is also served for lunch alongside soup or stew. Asho's family enjoys having canjeero in the morning, and as an accompaniment to *maraq* (see recipe, p. 83).

INGREDIENTS

2 cups milk

1 cup flour

1 cup Cream of Wheat (farina)

1 tablespoon sugar

½ teaspoon salt

3 teaspoons baking powder

1 egg

Water as needed

1. Place milk, flour, Cream of Wheat (farina), sugar, and salt in a blender and mix on high for 30 seconds.
2. Cover and leave in a warm place to ferment overnight.
3. In the morning, add baking powder and egg and blend to combine. Add water, if needed, to achieve the consistency of a pancake batter.
4. Heat a nonstick skillet over medium heat. Slowly ladle about ½ cup of batter into the pan in a spiral movement, starting in the middle and using the back of the ladle to create a pattern.
5. Cook the canjeero until bubbles form, 1–2 minutes. Cover and cook until done, about 30 seconds. It should be golden and spongy and fully cooked.
6. Serve warm, drizzled with butter, ghee, or sesame oil, and sugar. Typical serving is 3 per person.

Community Feasts and Flavors

MAIN DISHES AND HEARTY SOUPS

Laksa

Provided by Peter Ringold in collaboration with Maimun Hassan Ringold, ReWA Supporters

This lively Malaysian specialty includes several specialty ingredients that are worth seeking out. Galangal is a tuber similar to ginger or turmeric, but with a very different flavor. It has a harder texture with a sharp, piney flavor. If you can't find it fresh, you can substitute with 2–3 pieces of dried galangal rehydrated in hot water.

Belachan is a pungent dried shrimp paste that can be found in many Asian markets or online. It comes in a brick form and is usually roasted before using. A wet, Thai style shrimp paste can be substituted, but will deliver a slightly different, less smoky flavor. Finally, candle nuts are large, waxy nuts that can be found in most Asian food stores and must be cooked before eating. Cashews can be substituted.

INGREDIENTS

Broth
18 large prawns, shell on
½ cup vegetable oil
2 cups fresh laksa paste (recipe follows)
4 cups chicken stock
4 cups water
2 cups full-fat coconut milk
2 tablespoons palm or brown sugar
3 tablespoons salt
Juice of 1 lime
Tofu puffs (about 3–4 per serving),
    cut each tofu puff in half

6 servings of rice / vermicelli / rice stick /
    wheat noodles / hokkien noodles

Suggested Garnishes
Lime wedges
Cilantro leaves
Thinly sliced green onions
Mung bean sprouts
Sliced green or red chilis
Sambal or chili oil

1.   Shell and devein prawns, reserving shells.

2. Heat oil in a large soup pot over medium-high, and fry prawn shells for 1–2 minutes, or until they turn red and start to become translucent.
3. Remove shells from the oil and discard them; retain the oil.
4. To this flavored oil, add laksa paste and fry until fragrant.
5. Slowly pour in the stock and water; whisk to combine.
6. Bring to a boil and then add coconut milk, sugar, salt, and lime. Lower the heat and simmer for at least 20 minutes to let the flavors come out.
7. While the broth is simmering, blanch prawns in boiling water for about 4 minutes and set aside.
8. Using a fine mesh sieve or colander, strain the laksa broth. Return broth to soup pot, add tofu puffs and bring to a simmer over low heat.
9. Prepare noodles according to package instructions.
10. Serve in bowls; add noodles first, then broth, and top with prawns and desired garnishes.

Laksa Paste

1 large shallot, peeled and roughly chopped
5 cloves garlic, peeled and roughly chopped
3 stalks lemongrass, white part only, roughly chopped
3 inches galangal, peeled and roughly chopped
2 inches ginger, peeled

1 tablespoon belachan, dried shrimp paste
¾ cup vegetable oil
1 cup dried red chili (such as chili de arbol), stems removed, soaked in hot water
4 candle nuts (or ⅛ cup cashews)
1 tablespoon ground turmeric
1 tablespoon ground coriander
½ teaspoon ground white pepper

1. Place shallot, garlic, lemongrass, galangal, and ginger into a blender or food processor. Add remaining ingredients and process until mixture becomes a smooth, thick paste.

ANNIE

ReWA Development Officer • Vietnam

When my parents came to the US as refugees in 1975, they couldn't resume their respective careers as a naval officer and a schoolteacher. Instead, they reinvented themselves. My father worked toward acquiring degrees in engineering, and my mom opened her own restaurant—Mai's. Mai's was the only restaurant to serve Vietnamese food (and inspired French cuisine) in Mobile, Alabama, and for more than eight years, the restaurant not only employed my sister, aunt, and uncles, but provided enough to pay for their college tuition fees.

That didn't mean much for me, though. I was only seven when the restaurant opened, and growing up, I just longed for more time with my mom. She was often still sleeping when I had to leave the house for school, and after school she would only be home for an hour to prepare dinner for our family before going back to the restaurant.

On special occasions, the elegant dishes that Mai's was known for, like butterflied coconut shrimp or egg rolls, made it to our dinner plates, but *chao ga* is what I think of when I think about my mom. When I

make it for my daughter now, I always tell her about her *bà ngoai*'s (maternal grandmother's) restaurant and how our little refugee family in Mobile survived for years on love, hard work, and good food.

Yield: 8 servings

Chao Ga

Provided by Annie Nguyen, ReWA Development Officer

Served in all parts of Vietnam at all times of the day, chao ga is a rice porridge that is neither fancy nor particularly complex. Rather, it's the kind of dish you serve when your daughter is feeling lonely, when you want to be home but can't, when life is a little too complicated and you need to slow it down. The slow cooking over low heat results in a clear broth packed with rich flavor.

INGREDIENTS

1 whole chicken, 2–3 pounds

6 inches ginger root, peeled
    and cut into 3 pieces

1 stalk lemongrass, white
    part only, chopped

1 tablespoon salt

2 tablespoons uncooked jasmine rice

¼ cup cilantro leaves

¼ cup minced chives

½ teaspoon black ground pepper

1 lime, cut into 8 wedges

1. Wash chicken thoroughly. Place chicken with bones, skin, heart, liver, and gizzard in a large pot. Add chicken, ginger, lemongrass, and salt. Add water to cover and bring to a boil.

2. Reduce heat to just below a simmer, cover, and cook gently for 1 to 1½ hours.

3. Remove chicken and set aside. Strain broth and return to pot. Once chicken is cool enough to handle, remove and discard bones and skin, and tear meat into bite-size pieces.

4. Stir rice into broth and bring to a boil. Reduce heat to medium, and cook for 30–60 minutes, stirring occasionally. If necessary, add more water or salt. For a thicker dish, cook longer, as the consistency of the chau will become more porridge-like the longer the rice cooks with the broth.

5. Divide chau ga among eight bowls and top with chicken meat. Garnish with cilantro, chives, and pepper. Serve with lime wedges.

RAHIMA

ReWA Volunteer • Somalia

Not long after the civil war started in Somalia, a gang of men forced their way in to Rahima's home looking for money and jewelry. They made the girls and women of the household take off their headscarves so that nothing could be hidden. Fearing their safety, Rahima's mother took the children to stay with an aunt that very night. After a year, they moved with a family member to the relative stability and security of a village away from the city. The family never returned to live in their home in Mogadishu; it was simply too dangerous.

Shortly after that incident, Rahima's brother, then an older teen, fled to Kenya. It would be many years before she saw him again. During that time the family did not know whether he was dead or alive. There was no infrastructure—no phones or postal service—so people sent messages through travelers in hopes that they would reach their loved ones.

Miraculously, Rahima and her surviving family members received the good news that her brother made it to the US after spending several years in a refugee camp in Kenya. In 1999, at the age of sixteen and after two years of living in a Kenyan refugee camp, Rahima and several family members were able to join her brother in the US thanks to his sponsorship. They first joined him in San Jose, before moving to Minneapolis, then to Las Vegas, before finally settling in Seattle in 2009.

To this day, Rahima is haunted by images of war. "Every time I see war in the news, it takes me right back to the fear and sorrow I experienced in my country. I wish others would learn from what happened to us."

During her time in Las Vegas, Rahima didn't find much by way of community other than during birthday parties, when mothers and kids gathered and shared food and stories. Later, she enjoyed swapping recipes and making friends at ESL class potlucks. Over time, she came to be known for her talent as an excellent cook. Rahima was delighted when she was asked to share her skills and culture with her New Holly community in Seattle. Today, she teaches cooking to kids aged eight to fifteen. She hopes to share her passion for connecting people over food with her fellow adult students as well.

"Food brings people together. It says, 'this is who we are, this is our culture.' It keeps us connected to each other, and the places we come from."

Yield: 6 servings

Spiced Chicken

Provided by Rahima, ReWA Volunteer

This beautifully spiced dish is quick to put together, even on a weeknight, and is especially delicious when served with bariis, a Somali rice dish, just as Rahima does.

INGREDIENTS

1 tablespoon cumin seeds

1 teaspoon coriander seeds

1 teaspoon freshly ground black pepper

1 teaspoon ground paprika

1 teaspoon ground turmeric

¼ cup canola oil

1 teaspoon store-bought vegetable seasoning or chicken bouillon powder (optional)

2 onions, finely chopped

2 pounds boneless, skinless chicken breast or thighs, cut into 1-inch pieces

1 green pepper, thinly sliced

1 red pepper, thinly sliced

1 tablespoon chopped cilantro

1. Toast cumin and coriander seeds in a dry pan until fragrant and set aside until cool. Pulverize in a spice grinder or mortar and pestle.
2. In a small bowl, mix cumin, coriander, black pepper, paprika, and turmeric.
3. Heat oil in a large pan over medium heat. Add onion and sauté until translucent.
4. Add chicken and sauté until browned. Add spices, vegetable seasoning if using, and ½ cup water, and cook for 20 minutes.
5. Garnish with sweet peppers and cilantro.

Bariis

Provided by Rahima, ReWA Volunteer

Bariis is a festive dish that is served to guests or during special occasions, and it is one of the most popular rice dishes in Somalia. The warm spices provide a complexity and depth of flavor. Rahima uses goat broth in her recipe, which lends a traditional taste of home, but chicken or vegetable broth can be used as substitutes.

This is the very dish that launched *Recipes for Refuge*. Rahima taught a well-received cooking class for ReWA featuring this recipe, which planted the seed to share the stories, cultures, and foods of ReWA clients. Thank you, Rahima!

INGREDIENTS

Rice
3 cups basmati rice
1 teaspoon cumin seeds
1 teaspoon coriander seeds
¼ teaspoon cardamom seeds
1 teaspoon ground turmeric
1 cinnamon stick
½ teaspoon freshly ground black pepper
1 onion, diced

1 teaspoon minced garlic
¼ cup canola oil
2 tomatoes, chopped
Salt
2 teaspoons xawaash (recipe, p. 14)
1 tablespoon vegetable bouillon
     powder (optional)
6 cups goat broth (or substitute
     chicken or vegetable broth)

1. Soak the rice in cold water for 30 minutes, rinse thoroughly and drain.
2. Over medium-low heat, toast cumin, coriander, and cardamom seeds in a dry pan until fragrant. Transfer to a plate to cool and then pulverize in a spice grinder or with a mortar and pestle. Mix in turmeric, cinnamon, and black pepper.
3. Heat oil over medium heat in a large pan. Add onion and sauté, stirring frequently, until softened. Add garlic and cook; stir for about a minute. Add tomatoes and sauté for 5 minutes.

4. Remove mixture from the heat and puree in food processor. Return puree to the pan over medium heat along with rice and stir well. Add spices, xawaash, salt, and bouillon powder if using, and sauté for several minutes until fragrant. Add broth and bring to a boil. Cover and cook on low heat for 20 minutes

DEEQA

ReWA Employee • Somalia

In Mogadishu, Somalia, Deeqa's family lived a good life. Her father was an import/exporter, and Deeqa and her four siblings enjoyed playing with their toys and pets. Each child had a pet; Deeqa's was a chicken and her brother's was a rooster. Her first experience with death was when her chicken was hit by a car.

Deeqa was only three when the conflict started in Somalia in 1992. The family lost everything—their home and all their possessions—in one night. The banks were closed, and the family was only able to bring a few valuables with them, each family member carrying a small amount of gold in fanny packs. Although Deeqa's mother

was from a neutral tribe, her father's tribe was persecuted. Deeqa's uncle was killed in the conflict, but her family made it out of the country and lived for three years in a refugee camp in Kenya. Surrounded by fencing and guards, Deeqa's family lived with extended family members in a house made out of sticks and plastic bags. It consisted of a kitchen and one room for everyone to sleep in.

Deeqa's memories of being in the camp are mostly positive. She remembers playing with the other children, climbing mango trees, and playing with a soccer ball made of ripped-up clothes and socks. The children often played hide-and-seek or "bowled" using Coke bottles filled with sand as pins.

From the Kenyan refugee camp, the family made their way to Nairobi, where they were able to secure sponsorship to move to the US.

Deeqa remembers being thrilled at the idea of moving to America. In her mind, people in the US had robots working for them and everyone lived in big lavish houses and could have anything they wanted. The reality was less rosy.

The family arrived in the middle of winter without coats or jackets. The long flight from Nairobi to New York was made even worse when Deeqa and two of her sisters became ill from the unfamiliar airplane food. After a night in New York City, they landed in Tennessee, where they lived for several months before traveling to Seattle. In Seattle, they were greeted by her mother's family members, who had sponsored them, as well as neighbors from Mogadishu. The reunion after so many years was very emotional.

Deeqa attended Maple Elementary, where many Somali children were also students, but then she moved on to another school, where she was one of just a few kids from Somalia. There, a classmate saw her wearing a hijab and asked if she was bald. Deeqa would go on to attend many schools. Through it all, she still felt like the new girl—the girl who was different.

After completing her associate's degree, Deeqa applied to work at ReWA, where her mother had taken ESL classes and found support during those first months and years in Seattle. She remembered ReWA as a place that supported women during a time of profound change.

Hilib Ari

Provided by Deeqa Alibarre, ReWA Youth Case Manager & Family Advocate

Usually served with rice, *hilib ari* is a lovely way to eat goat and a popular dish in Somali households. Halal grocery stores usually carry frozen goat meat, and some halal markets and specialty butchers offer fresh goat meat as well. This is one of Deeqa's favorite meals made by her mother.

INGREDIENTS

2 pounds goat meat
1 tablespoon olive oil
1 large onion, chopped
½ green bell pepper, diced
½ red bell pepper, diced
2 teaspoons salt
1 teaspoon ground pepper
1 teaspoon minced garlic

1 teaspoon minced ginger
½ teaspoon ground cumin
3 whole cloves, crushed
4 cardamom seeds, crushed
½ teaspoon ground cinnamon
¼ cup fresh cilantro leaves
Juice of ½ lemon

1. Rinse meat and drain.
2. Fill a large stock pot with water and add about 1 tablespoon salt. Add meat, bring to a boil, then lower to a simmer. Cook for about 2 hours or until meat is tender.
3. Drain meat and set aside to cool. When cool, cut into 2-inch cubes.
4. Add olive oil to a large skillet set over medium-high heat. When the oil is hot, add the meat and sear on all sides.
5. Add onions and bell peppers. Sauté for about 3 minutes, or until slightly softened but still vibrant.
6. Add 2 teaspoons salt, pepper, garlic, ginger, cumin, cloves, cardamom, and cinnamon. Cook for roughly 2 minutes, stirring to combine the flavors.
7. Remove from heat. Stir in cilantro and lemon juice.

STEPHANIE

ReWA Administrative Assistant to the Executive Director • Cambodia

Stephanie was only four years old when she emigrated from Cambodia to the US with her large family as refugees. She had already overcome many hurdles in her short life. As a baby, she had fallen very ill and spent weeks in a coma. Her father was in the army fighting the Khmer Rouge at the time, and as the Cambodian forces lost ground, their family home-life became more perilous. Her parents fled the country to the relative safety of a refugee camp in Thailand. Before the UNHCR resettled her family to the US, they spent time in a second refugee camp in the Philippines.

"My family came to America with no knowledge of the language or culture. I heard many stories from my parents about the hardships they endured, but also how much they appreciated the opportunities provided to us in our new country.

"I have interpreted for my parents ever since I was young, but my parents always emphasized how important it was for me to have an education. They wanted me to succeed and have the ability to support myself, and for that, I am so grateful to them.

"I know firsthand that struggling with few resources and limited English can be very overwhelming and stressful for all members of a family, so I am happy to work for an organization that connects immigrants and refugees with the services they need to make them feel they are not alone. I am blessed to be able to work at ReWA."

Stephanie earned her associate's degree in sociology with a minor in business. She joined the ReWA staff in 2000 and worked her way up to the position of administrative assistant to the executive director. She and her husband, also a refugee from Cambodia, have three children.

Yao Hon

Provided by Stephanie Rim, ReWA Administrative Assistant to the Executive Director

Stephanie loves hot pot, known as *yao hon* or *chhnang pleurng* ("fire pot" in Cambodian), because it brings people together.

Like many Cambodian recipes, this relies on *kroeung* or lemongrass paste, which is typically made fresh every day in a mortar and pestle. This can also be quickly made in a food processor. Two ingredients might need to be sourced at Asian food stores. These include Coco Loco, a brand of coconut soda, and Chinese barbecue sauce, which may have a "for hot pot" indicator on the label. It comes in regular and spicy flavors and either variety works. Some popular brands are Dragonfly (usually in a glass jar) and Bull Head (comes in a silver can).

INGREDIENTS

Lemongrass Paste / Kroeung

2 stalks lemongrass, white part only, sliced

2 shallots, peeled and chopped

2-inch piece of galangal, peeled and chopped

2-inch piece of ginger, peeled and chopped

5 cloves garlic, peeled

4 lime leaves

5 bird's eye chilis

1 tablespoon turmeric powder

1 tablespoon paprika

4 tablespoons water

Broth

2 (13.5-ounce) cans full-fat coconut milk

2 (13.5-ounce) cans water (use coconut milk cans to measure the water)

2 (14.5-ounce) cans chicken stock

Lemongrass paste (see recipe)

1 jar Chinese barbecue sauce

1 (12-ounce) can Coco Rico (may substitute lemon-lime soda)

1 tablespoon or 1 cube granulated chicken bouillon

¼ cup grated palm sugar (brown sugar can be used as a substitute)

Juice of 1 lime

¼ cup fish sauce

Dipping Sauce

4 bird's eye chilis, stemmed
and thinly sliced
4 cloves garlic, peeled and minced

⅓ cup lime juice
⅓ cup fish sauce
⅓ cup sugar

FOR DIPPING

Vegetables

Any variety of greens (watercress, spinach,
baby bok choy, basil leaves, cilantro,
chrysanthemum leaves, pea shoots,
yam leaves, mustard greens, etc.)
Chinese broccoli, trimmed
Napa cabbage, cut into thin wedges
Taro, blanched and sliced
Mushrooms, stemmed and sliced
(any variety, such as buttons,
oyster, enoki, shiitake, etc.)
Green beans, stemmed
Tomatoes, cut into wedges

Proteins

Thinly sliced beef
Asian premade meatballs
Fried bean curd sheets
Tofu puffs
Firm tofu cubes
Quail eggs
Shrimp, peeled and deveined
Squid, cleaned and cut into bite-size pieces
Imitation crab meat chunks
Fish balls / fish cake

EQUIPMENT

There are a few ways to set up a hot pot at home. The most common way is to use an electric burner or hot plate to heat the pot in the center of the dining table. If you do not have this type of setup, you can use a slow cooker, rice cooker, or multi-cooker. However, the broth must be kept at a simmer if you are cooking meats and seafood.

1. To make lemongrass paste, place all the ingredients in the bowl of a food processor and blend until a rough paste forms.
2. In a large pot, bring coconut milk, water, and chicken stock to a boil over high heat. Lower the heat to medium and simmer for 3–4 minutes. Add the remaining broth ingredients and simmer for 20 minutes.
3. While the broth is simmering, prepare noodles or rice according to the instructions. Each diner will have noodles or rice as a base to eat with the hot pot ingredients and broth. Any type of noodles or rice can be used.

4. To make the dipping sauce, stir together all ingredients until the sugar dissolves.
5. Wash and prepare vegetables, seafood, meats, and other ingredients for the filling.
6. Place ingredients for the filling in communal dishes so that all diners can access them and take part in cooking them. Provide each diner with a dish for the dipping sauce too.
7. Transfer the broth to your hot pot (or alternative vessel) in the center of the table and wait for it to simmer, then start adding meats first, followed by seafood, and lastly, vegetables. For sanitary purposes, it's best to designate separate utensils to pick up raw meat and seafood to place into the simmering broth. Have several spider strainers, ladles, and tongs on hand to fish out cooked ingredients. It may take several batches or rounds of cooking to get through the meal.

If you have leftover broth and fillings, consider making a soup for another meal!

Yield: About 1 cup

Berbere

Provided by Betina Simmons Blaine, ReWA Bridge Builder Volunteer

The word *berbere* means "hot" in Amharic and, as the name suggests, it is traditionally quite spicy! This is the spice mixture that provides delicious layers of flavor and heat as well as a rich brick-red color to dishes like doro wat and misir wat. There are many variations, and you can certainly reduce the amount of chili if you want less heat. Prepared berbere is also available in most Ethiopian and Eritrean markets.

INGREDIENTS

5 dried red chilis (such as arbol),
    stemmed, seeded, and crumbled
2 teaspoons coriander seeds
2 teaspoons cumin seeds
1 teaspoon fenugreek seeds
½ teaspoon whole black peppercorns
¼ teaspoon whole allspice
6 black cardamom pods

4 cloves
3 tablespoons paprika (hot or mild)
2 teaspoons kosher salt
1 teaspoon ground turmeric
½ teaspoon ground nutmeg
½ teaspoon ground ginger
½ teaspoon ground cinnamon

1. Toast the chilis and whole spices over low heat in a dry skillet until fragrant, being careful not to burn.
2. Allow whole spices to cool. Grind them in a spice grinder or with a mortar and pestle until fine.
3. Transfer to a bowl and stir in paprika, salt, turmeric, nutmeg, ginger, and cinnamon. Store in an airtight container.

AMINA

SeaTac ESL Student • Afghanistan

Amina arrived in Seattle with her husband and children in 2017 from the beautiful Panjshir Valley, a three-hour drive north of Kabul. She loved her home in Panjshir where her husband had a horse, the air was clean, and the family was relatively safe from the battles of Kabul. However, Amina's husband's work as an interpreter for the US forces forced the family to move to Kabul. The Taliban threatened to shoot anyone cooperating with or helping the US, putting her husband and family in a perilous position. Her family had to seek asylum in the US for their safety. Her husband now works as a driver for Amazon, and also as a taxi driver.

While Amina appreciates being safe in the US, she desperately misses the country and family she left behind. In Afghanistan, she had a home in Kabul and a home near her mother in Panjshir. Here, she resides in a two-bedroom apartment with her family of eight. Since moving to the US, Amina's twenty-nine-year-old brother was killed while breaking up a fight in India, where he was studying for his master's degree. Her mother was hospitalized in Iran, because of the lack of healthcare options at home. It was painful for Amina to be so far away from her family during these times. Amina wishes she were able to be near them. She hopes to someday return to her beloved home in Panjshir.

Yield: 4–6 servings

Chapli Kebab

Provided by Amina, ReWA Student

Different from the cubed-meat skewers that "kebab" means to many westerners, this minced meat dish is a popular part of both Afghan and Pakistani cuisine. The name is thought to come from the word for "flat" or "sandal." Amina prefers to pan-fry her *chapli* kebab, though it can also be grilled. Like many recipes, there are many variations—some add ginger, chili flakes, cinnamon, and even pomegranate seeds. This is often served with *qabli* for celebrations.

INGREDIENTS

2 pounds ground or minced
  beef, lamb, or chicken
1 large yellow onion, grated
2 carrots, grated
1 russet potato, peeled and grated
1 chili pepper, finely chopped
1 clove garlic, finely chopped

2 eggs, beaten
¼ cup flour
1 cup fresh cilantro, finely chopped
1–2 teaspoons salt
¼ teaspoon ground black pepper
½–1 teaspoon garam masala
¼ cup vegetable oil, for frying

1. Place all ingredients except for the vegetable oil into a medium bowl. Mix ingredients by hand, and knead for several minutes until thoroughly combined.
2. Divide mixture into golf-sized balls and flatten into patties.
3. Heat the oil in skillet over medium-high heat.
4. Drop the patties one by one into the hot oil.
5. Fry until the meat is cooked and golden brown, several minutes per side.

Yield: 6 servings

Doro Wat

Provided by Maaza and Saba, ReWA Students

Doro wat is a spicy, richly flavored chicken and onion stew from Eritrea and Ethiopia. It is a perfect gateway to Eritrean and Ethiopian cuisine because it looks and tastes complex, yet it isn't very difficult to make. Berbere—the warm spice mix including chilis, cardamom, fenugreek, cumin, ginger, paprika, and more—is prominently featured in this dish. You can purchase or make your own berbere (see recipe, p. 58), along with the spiced butter known as *niter kibbeh* (recipe follows).

INGREDIENTS

6–8 bone-in chicken thighs

3 tablespoons niter kibbeh (oil or ghee can be used as substitutes)

3 onions, finely chopped

2–3 tablespoons berbere, depending on your spice tolerance

1 tablespoon garlic, finely chopped

½ tablespoon ginger, finely grated

1 tablespoon tomato paste

½ teaspoon smoked paprika

2–3 cups water

6 soft-boiled eggs, peeled

Juice of 1 lemon

Salt and pepper

1. Score chicken skin and season with salt and pepper. Set aside.
2. Heat a large pot on medium heat. Add niter kibbeh, ghee, or oil. Add onions and sauté until they begin to brown, at least 10 minutes.
3. Add berbere, garlic, and ginger. Cook, stirring, for several minutes until fragrant.
4. Add tomato paste and paprika. Cook, stirring, for 2–3 minutes to combine.
5. Add the chicken, and then enough water to cover. Simmer for 30 minutes or until the chicken is cooked through.
6. Add eggs and continue to cook for 10 minutes.
7. Add lemon juice, salt, and pepper.
8. Serve warm with injera or rice.

Yield: About 1 cup

Niter Kibbeh

Provided by Betina Simmons Blaine, ReWA Bridge Builder Volunteer

This clarified butter infused with spices is common in Ethiopian and Eritrean cuisine. It adds an unmistakable depth of flavor and a taste that is unique to the region. There are many variations, so feel free to experiment with the optional spices. While ghee or oil can be substituted in the dishes that contain niter kibbeh, ReWA volunteer Betina found that this easy recipe is well worth making for delicious and authentic results. If you prefer, niter kibbeh is available in East African specialty food markets.

INGREDIENTS

½ teaspoon whole cardamom seeds
2 sticks unsalted butter
½ yellow onion, finely chopped
2 to 3 garlic cloves, minced
1 tablespoon grated fresh ginger
½ teaspoon coarsely ground black pepper
¼ teaspoon ground turmeric

Optional
1 cinnamon stick
1 clove
½ teaspoon coriander seeds
¼ teaspoon cumin seeds
¼ teaspoon ground nutmeg
¼ teaspoon fenugreek seeds
¼ teaspoon nigella seeds

1. Toast the whole spices over low heat in a dry skillet just until fragrant. Transfer to a bowl to stop cooking.
2. Place the butter in a small saucepan and melt over low heat.
3. Add remaining ingredients and simmer over very low heat for about an hour. Do not allow it to burn.
4. You will see that the butter has separated into a clear liquid on top with milk solids at the bottom. Strain through cheesecloth to remove all solids and discard.
5. Store spiced clarified butter in a refrigerator or a freezer.

Pho Ga

Provided by Thu-Van Nguyen, ReWA Founding Mother

Pho Ga is a popular Vietnamese chicken noodle soup. The traditional noodles are long rice sticks, and the combination of pho spices and fish sauce create a unique and savory flavor. Traditionally eaten with chopsticks, each mouthful of the soft, warm noodles is a comforting bite of home for Thu-Van's family. While there are many varieties of pho, Thu-Van's adult children have always been particularly fond of their mother's pho ga. If you're feeding pho to young children, as do many Vietnamese mothers, use a clean pair of kitchen scissors to cut up the long noodles into more child-friendly portions.

Thu-Van's husband is Jewish. While his mother, Frances Oliver Loud, was alive, she loved Thu-Van's cooking. When Mrs. Loud grew elderly and frail, Thu-Van's family moved her into a Jewish nursing home. One of her most frequent complaints, though, was the home would not allow food from outside to be brought on site. To satisfy Mrs. Loud's cravings, Thu-Van and her husband regularly brought her home with them for a dinner of Jewish matzo ball soup with a Vietnamese touch that she so adored and missed. Hint: for an all-American cross-cultural experience, add some fish sauce to your matzo ball soup next Passover, but don't tell the rabbis we told you to do it.

INGREDIENTS

Stock

1 medium stewing hen
1 pound chicken breast
2 medium onions, peeled and broiled in
    oven until well browned on all sides
4 inches of ginger, peeled and broiled in
    oven until well browned on all sides
1 medium jicama, peeled and diced
1 small daikon radish, peeled and diced
5 whole star anise (40 "points" total)

6 whole cloves
3-inch cinnamon stick
1½ tablespoons salt
1 ounce (about 1 inch) chunk
    of yellow rock sugar (may
    substitute with other sugars)
4 tablespoons fish sauce (preferably
    the 3 Crabs brand of nuoc mam)

Bowls

2 pounds thin dried or fresh *banh pho* noodles ("rice sticks" or Thai *chantaboon*)

4 green onions, green part only, thinly sliced

Fresh ground black pepper

Optional Garnishes

Bean sprouts, washed and drained

Hoisin sauce

Cilantro leaves, washed, drained, and chopped

Lime wedges

Asian basil

Chili pepper, thinly sliced (Thai, dragon, or jalapeño)

Spearmint

1. Bring 3 quarts of water to a boil in a deep stockpot. Reduce heat to a simmer.
2. Add whole chicken and chicken breasts. Reduce heat to the point where you see only a few bubbles rise to the surface, skim off any foam that collects on the surface.
3. Add onions, ginger, jicama, daikon, star anise, cloves, cinnamon, salt, sugar, and fish sauce.
4. After 10 minutes, use a ladle or tongs to remove chicken breasts. Place them in a saucepan on the stove and add just enough of the broth to cover them completely. Heat till barely simmering, then immediately turn off the heat and cover. Remove the breasts when just cooked through, about 10 more minutes. Transfer the broth from the saucepan back to the large stock pot. Set aside the chicken breasts.
5. Continue to cook the broth at a low simmer, halfway covered. Occasionally stir and remove any foam that rises to the surface. Total cooking time for the broth is about 2 hours. When the stock is ready, drain liquid through a colander. Discard all solids.
6. When chicken breasts are cool, use two forks to shred the meat.
7. Bring a pot of water to a boil to prepare the noodles. If using dry noodles, add 1 teaspoon mild oil to the boiling water along with the noodles. When they become medium soft, drain and rinse under cold water. If using fresh noodles, add to boiling water. As soon as water returns to a simmer, remove from the heat and drain right away.
8. In each individual bowl, place the noodles and top with shredded chicken meat, green onions, and a sprinkle of freshly ground black pepper. Pour in the broth. Serve at the table with garnishes for each diner to add to their bowls as they wish.

MBUKA

SeaTac ESL Student • Democratic Republic of Congo

Mbuka grew up in Kinshasa, the largest and capital city of the Democratic Republic of Congo (DRC). When she was twenty years old, she moved to Lubango, Angola, where she worked in a Congolese restaurant for ten years.

In 2018, Mbuka came to the US, landing first in Texas before moving to Seattle, where she lives with her two boys. She attends school from Monday to Thursday and on Friday she volunteers in the ReWA preschool on Beacon Hill. And she still likes to cook!

Yield: 4–6 servings

Poisson de Mer with Cassava and Pap

Provided by Mbuka, ReWA ESL Student

Poisson de mer translates simply as "fish of the sea" or saltwater fish, though you can use any white fish. This tasty tilapia dish, accompanied by cornmeal mush and cassava, is one Mbuka cooked every day in Angola. It is also very popular in her native country of DRC. Pap goes by many names in different African countries. The firm mush is commonly used to dip into and scoop up sauces and stews.

INGREDIENTS

1 whole tilapia, scaled and cleaned

1 teaspoon salt

1 teaspoon turmeric

1 teaspoon ground red pepper
   (aleppo or cayenne)

1 medium onion, peeled and cut in chunks

2 stalks celery, cut in chunks

4 cloves garlic, peeled

Small piece of ginger (1 inch by
   1 inch), peeled and cut in chunks

Juice of ½ lemon

Oil for frying

1. Wash the fish and pat dry. Put in a shallow baking dish.
2. The fish can be prepared either as a whole piece or in pieces. To prepare in pieces, cut the fish in 4; cut a slit about 2 inches into each piece and return to the bowl. To prepare the whole fish, make three to four parallel slits into the fish body on the back and belly, between the head and the tail, using a sharp knife. Don't cut so deep that you separate the pieces of the fish. Repeat on remaining side. Return fish to the baking dish.
3. Put remaining ingredients into a blender or food processor and blend into a paste. Cover the fish with this paste, working the mixture into the slits. Cover and let it marinate for 10–15 minutes.

4. In a large frying pan or heavy-bottomed pot, add enough oil to fry fish (about 2 inches deep). Heat the oil over medium heat until it reaches 330–350 degrees. Carefully lower the fish into the oil and cook on one side for 5 minutes, and then turn and cook for another 4–5 minutes.

Cassava

2 (24-ounce) packages of frozen cassava pieces (also called yuca or manioc)

1 medium eggplant, cubed

2 small zucchini, sliced

1 large onion, peeled and chopped

4 large cloves garlic, peeled and minced

½ cup vegetable oil

1 teaspoon salt

¼ teaspoon nutmeg

1. Place all the ingredients in a large pot. Cover and cook for 20 minutes over low heat without stirring. You want the ingredients to simmer slowly, rather than boil. After 20 minutes, stir again. At this point, all the vegetables should be cooked down to a homogenous mixture.

Pap

2 cups water

2 cups finely milled white corn flour*

1. In a medium saucepan, bring the water to a boil. Meanwhile, in a separate bowl, mix a little water with 1 cup of the corn flour to make a thick paste.
2. Add this mixture to the boiling water and cook for 10 minutes, stirring frequently.
3. Slowly add the remaining cup of corn flour, stirring constantly, and continue stirring until the mixture is thick and holds its shape. Allow to cool slightly and roll into palm-sized balls to serve.

*Note: The flour used for pap is sometimes found under the brand name Pan and can be found at import stores. You can use white masa harina as a substitute, but don't use coarse-ground corn such as polenta or cornmeal.

MAHNAZ

ReWA Executive Director, 2013–present • Iran

ReWA students, clients, staff members, volunteers, and Founding Mothers have shared their journey stories here, so it feels important that I be willing to share mine with you, as well.

I was twenty years old when I first arrived in the US. I remember the pride in knowing I had come to attend an American college and receive the best education in the world. Before that day, I had never been outside of Iran without my parents, nor had I ever been away from my mother or father for any significant length of time. My excitement, optimism, and intense drive to excel in school helped quiet the butterflies. Still, you never truly overcome the challenges that accompany being more than 7,000 miles away from family and friends.

Little did I know, though, how much more difficult the experience was going to become for me.

I would never again set foot in my home country, never again see some of the most important people in my life.

You see, just six months after arriving in the US, the Iranian Revolution began—a conflict that saw the violent overthrow of the government and the rise of an anti-Western authoritarian regime.

For much of those early days of the Revolution, life was almost unbearable. The uncertainty. The anxiety. And, honestly, it became even harder before things got better. While I was never able to return to Iran, for a variety of reasons, my father was never able to leave the country.

Thankfully, my mother and two sisters were eventually able to join me. I had become a US citizen and was allowed to sponsor them for permanent residency. It wasn't until they arrived, though, that I really felt like I could begin to rebuild my life here.

I remember that day distinctly, how excited I was to see my mother. It had been five years already. But my heart dropped when I caught my first glimpse of her at the airport. My very poised, beautiful mother looked as though she had aged at least twenty years. I couldn't stop crying. Later on, I learned the terrible details of what she had endured during the revolution and during the Iran-Iraq war. Those horror stories haunt me to this day.

In Iran, my mother had been quite successful. She had a professional career and a happy, healthy family. It was very difficult for her to start all over again once she came to the US, but she adjusted graciously. Rather than return to the work world, she helped my sister and me raise our children. She taught them about the value of being bicultural and the importance of developing a successful career and contributing to society.

I graduated from college then went on to receive a master's degree in economics, as well as an MBA. I had a very successful career in the banking industry and raised two beautiful daughters. Once my girls had grown, I decided to change career paths and dedicate my working life to serving refugee and immigrant families.

My story is not very different from the stories of many of the refugees and immigrants that we serve at ReWA. It is the story of revolution, war, heartbreak, hard work, integration, triumph, joy, and the gratitude of being here and the opportunity to become an American.

Yes, my work at ReWA is personal. I have lived through the experience of being far from the home I love, and of creating a new life in a new country. I share this experience with our ReWA clients and know how critical it is for those of us living through this challenge to find a support network. I am truly honored to help build that scaffold of support for the families who seek services at ReWA.

Yield: 4 servings

Pomegranate Khoresh with Chicken

Provided by Mahnaz Eshetu, ReWA Executive Director

Traditionally, a formal Persian meal begins with lavash—thin, unleavened bread—feta cheese, herbs, and a sweet fruit or berry preserve. A khoresh would be served as part of the second course, along with saffron rice and yogurt. Mahnaz enjoys making a complete meal like this to celebrate the Persian New Year, honor special houseguests, and mark family birthdays and anniversaries.

Pomegranate molasses or paste is available in gourmet food markets and online, and is made in Iran and other Middle Eastern countries. Persian brands are much sweeter than most other brands. Mahnaz uses only Persian brands. If unable to find pomegranate paste, substitute with 4 cups pomegranate juice and eliminate water in the recipe (2½ cups). Mahnaz sometimes serves this topped with a roast chicken for a crowd (pictured), and always with saffron rice.

INGREDIENTS

5 tablespoons olive oil, divided
2 large onions, peeled and thinly sliced
2 pounds boneless, skinless
    chicken breast meat, cubed
1 teaspoon salt
½ cup shredded apple
½ cup shredded carrot
1 cup pomegranate molasses (also
    called pomegranate paste)

2½ cups water
2 cups shelled walnuts, finely ground
½ teaspoon cinnamon
¼ teaspoon ground saffron dissolved
    in 1 tablespoon hot water,
    plus a pinch for garnish
Seeds of a whole, fresh pomegranate

1. Heat 3 tablespoons olive oil in an ovenproof Dutch oven on the stove over medium heat. Brown onions and chicken. Add salt after browning.

2. Heat 2 tablespoons olive oil in a separate pan. Sauté shredded apples and carrots until apples are golden brown. Add to Dutch oven.

3. Dissolve pomegranate molasses in 2½ cups of water.

4. In a food processor, mix the walnuts with pomegranate molasses, cinnamon, and saffron water. The result should be a creamy paste. Add to Dutch oven.

5. Stir mixture in Dutch oven. Cover and simmer for 1½ hours. Stir occasionally to prevent scorching.

6. As stew thickens, add warm water to achieve desired consistency. Adjust saltiness, sweetness, and sourness.

7. Leave covered. Remove from the stove and keep warm in an oven until it is ready to be served.

8. Garnish with fresh pomegranate seeds and saffron just prior to serving.

GEORGE "GEO"

*Owner of Hood Famous Bakeshop and Cafe + Bar • California /
Second-Generation American with Filipino Parents*

George "Geo" Quibuyen is a rapper and spoken-word artist. He is one half of the acclaimed Seattle hip-hop group, Blue Scholars. He performs under the stage name Prometheus Brown.

Although Geo was born in California, his parents are Filipino immigrants. He and his wife, Chera, have two children, and they are the owners of Hood Famous Bakeshop in Ballard and Hood Famous Cafe + Bar in the International District. ReWA was thrilled when Geo emceed the 1st Annual ReWA Rock for Refuge at the Fremont Abbey in 2018.

Geo has spent his career as an artist elevating the value of cultural diversity. As the host of Seattle Crosscut's series "Kuya Geo," he muses on the issues of assimilation and cultural competence. The following is a brief summary of ideas he expressed in "The Generational Zigs and Zags of Immigrant Identity" episode, which aired in November 2018. Its themes are very relevant to the families being served at ReWA.

"I'm a child of Filipino immigrants, and I'm a father of young Filipino children. I've been thinking a lot about what it means to be Filipino, as a second generation Filipino American. How does identity change over time from one generation to the next? How do our ethnic identities get watered down over time? Who gets to be American and who is, instead, a perpetual foreigner? Most of all, I think of where exactly is home."

Sinigang

Provided by George "Geo" Quibuyen, rapper, spoken-word artist, and co-owner of Hood Famous Bakeshop and Hood Famous Cafe + Bar

Geo Quibuyen loves nearly every one of the many variations of *sinigang*—a Filipino sour meat and vegetable soup served with rice. Some use beef or shrimp as the main protein, some use guava or tamarind as the souring agent. Some are heavy on the bitter greens, some have little greens and more of the hearty plants. Some combine it all.

The sinigang variation he loves most is the simple one he grew up having, and that includes tamarind, pork feet, and mustard greens. Although other parts of the pig, like ribs or belly, can create a more flavorful, hearty sinigang, this version with pork feet and hocks is how his family had it most—back when the off-cuts were cheap and plentiful, before more recent culinary trends hiked their prices. Any greens will work, but mustard greens or *kangkong* (water spinach)—also the cheapest among the available greens in the market—add a signature bitterness to the sourness of the *sabaw* (soup).

It wasn't always Geo's favorite, though. "Honestly, I was forced to eat it, sometimes, when I would ungratefully ask why we weren't having spaghetti or mac and cheese or even other Filipino dishes that I liked better, like chicken adobo. But over time, not only did it become more delicious, but it also carried many dinnertime memories with it, like the times that my grandmother would collect the bones from all her grandchildren's finished plates to suck out any leftover bone marrow. Or plucking out one of the pig's thick leg hairs out of the fat that somehow made it past the butchering process. Or even the smell of it cooking, filling the house with an aroma that would last until the next morning."

INGREDIENTS

5 pounds pork hocks and feet (another cut can be substituted for feet)

4 quarts water

1 tablespoon oil (canola or refined coconut oil works well)

1 large white onion, diced

3 cloves garlic, peeled and crushed

4 Roma tomatoes, quartered

1 quart of rice wash (the water used to wash the starch from raw rice)

1 large daikon radish

2 bundles of bitter greens (mustard greens or kangkong are the best, but kale, chard, or collard greens can be substituted)

1 bundle of string beans

1 cup tamarind concentrate*

A dash of fish sauce (preferably Patis brand)

1 tablespoon salt

Ground black pepper

1 cup okra (optional)

1 eggplant, sliced (optional)

2–3 pieces chili (optional)

1. Turn off your phone or set it to vibrate, and put it somewhere where it won't distract you from the glorious act of preparing this dish.
2. Rinse and dry the pork. Heat a heavy pot over high heat and sear the pork. Transfer to a plate.
3. Add water into a pot and bring it to a boil. Add the pork back into the pot. Reduce to a simmer. Thank the pig for being a part of this dish and put on some good music.
4. In a separate pan, heat the oil over medium-high heat and sauté onions and garlic just until lightly browned (do not let it burn). Add tomatoes and stir for 1–2 minutes. Deglaze with rice wash, and let it simmer on medium-low heat for 4–5 minutes. Turn off heat and set aside.
5. Check on the simmering pork and skim off fat or impurities that have risen. Add more water if needed to keep the pork submerged.
6. Now would be a good time to peel and slice the daikon into rounds or half-rounds, wash and stem the greens, trim green beans, and dance, while the pork simmers.
7. After 30 minutes, add the contents of the deglazed pan, sliced daikon, tamarind concentrate, and salt to the pot containing the pork. Simmer until the pork is tender to your liking. Note that if you are using feet, this may take several hours.
8. Once the pork is tender, add string beans (and okra, eggplant, and chili if you wish).
9. Once the string beans (and veggies if you've added them) are tender, after about 10–15 minutes, stir in the bitter greens and turn off the heat. If using harder greens like kale or collard greens, let it simmer for 5–7 more minutes. Thank the farmers and workers who made all the ingredients available. Celebrate.
10. Add fish sauce, ground black pepper, and more tamarind.

*Note: Tamarind is the sticky brown pulp from the pod of a tree and is used widely in Asian cooking. The sour flavor it adds is unique and prized among Asian chefs. While tamarind concentrate is available ready-made in Asian food markets or online, you can make your own preservative-free, fresh tamarind concentrate by boiling equal parts tamarind pulp and water for 20–30 minutes, cooling and mashing, then separating the liquid from the pulp using a fine colander. Discard pulp after draining and use fresh liquid concentrate.

NI NI

ReWA SeaTac Student • Burma

Despite a harrowing journey to get here, Ni Ni emphasizes that she and her husband are now in a very happy place. Their circuitous immigration route took them from Burma to Malaysia, then Hong Kong to Los Angeles, until they arrived here in the Pacific Northwest. They are content to be living in the US today, and are thankful for the support they receive in this community. The best thing about their life is that Ni Ni feels safe living in SeaTac, Washington.

During their life together, Ni Ni and her husband have not always been this happy or felt so safe. They are members of a small population of Christian Burmese people, the "Karen," who have been persecuted by other groups living in Burma. When they were a newly married couple living in their home country, they faced nightmarish conditions. Ni Ni's husband was kidnapped, beaten, and forced into slavery. He lives with the debilitating back injuries from those beatings to this day.

Eventually, he escaped from his captors, but could not return home to live with Ni Ni as that would have endangered both of their lives. Instead, he found a passage to Malaysia, where he had to live a discreet life. It would be two years before Ni Ni could join him. While they were in Malaysia, they registered as refugees with the UNHCR and were thrilled when they eventually received permission to settle in the US.

Before fleeing Burma, Ni Ni owned a cosmetics sales business with an extensive client list. She went to her clients' homes and offices to demonstrate new products. Ni Ni is a smart and savvy woman; these traits have served her very well since she arrived here in US.

English as a Second Language (ESL) teachers at ReWA assess their students' language skills according to a leveling system, with Level One being the most rudimentary level. When Ni Ni arrived, her English ability was at Level One. Today, Ni Ni celebrates her language progress and achievements, and is a Level Seven student—the most advanced level in ESL classes ReWA can accommodate. If Ni Ni decides to continue studying English, her next step will be to enroll in an English program in the Seattle College system.

Ni Ni already has a stable job working at the Alki Bakery in Kent making sandwiches, veggie wraps, and fruit salads. While her employer and all of her colleagues are warm and friendly, she feels a particular affinity to one of her colleagues, who, like Ni Ni, arrived in this country as a refugee.

Mohinga

Provided by Ni Ni, ReWA Student

Mohinga, an earthy and vibrant fish soup, is considered by many to be the national dish of Burma. It is widely available from street vendors, and is most often eaten for breakfast. As with other typical Burmese dishes, the condiments are half the fun. You can add heat, acid, herbal notes, crunch, and texture to customize this soup to your liking. Ni Ni often brings this dish to her ESL-class potlucks, or to share with her colleagues for holiday gatherings.

INGREDIENTS

Thickener
1 cup dried yellow split peas (also called *chana dal* or split yellow gram)
4 cups water
½ teaspoon salt

Broth
1 stalk lemongrass, white part only
2-inch knob of ginger
1 teaspoon salt
½ teaspoon turmeric
10 cups cold water
1½–2 pounds whole pompano, cleaned and scaled (other white fish may be used such as catfish, snapper, or tilapia)

Soup
Neutral oil such as peanut or canola
3 cloves garlic, peeled and pounded or minced
2-inch knob of ginger, pounded or minced
2 stalks lemongrass, white part only, pounded or minced
1 tablespoon paprika
1 tablespoon mild chili powder
½ teaspoon turmeric
2 teaspoons shrimp paste
⅓ cup fish sauce
1 red onion, sliced
Salt
10 ounces vermicelli rice noodles

Suggested Garnishes
Hard-boiled eggs
Lime wedges

Fried shallots   Cilantro leaves
Chopped yard-long beans or green beans   Chili oil or chili flakes
Pe kyaw (split pea crackers)

1. To make thickener, boil split peas in 4 cups of water for 45–50 minutes over medium-high heat or until soft. You may need to add more water before cooking time ends, so check water level periodically to avoid scorching.
2. Once peas are tender, strain excess liquid, then season with about ½ teaspoon of salt.
3. Cover and set aside.
4. To make the broth, in a large pot, add all the broth ingredients except the fish. Bring to a boil over high heat.
5. Gently lower fish into the pot and lower to medium-high heat. Simmer for 15–20 minutes or until flesh pulls away easily from the bones.
6. Remove fish to cool, and reserve the poaching liquid.
7. Strain liquid through fine mesh strainer and set aside. Discard solids.
8. When the fish is cool enough to touch, remove all the flesh, cover, and set aside for later use. Discard all the skin and bones.
9. Wash the pot for the next step.
10. To make the soup, in a blender or food mill, add reserved thickener and a ladle or two of reserved poaching broth. Blend until smooth.
11. In the soup pot, heat 2 tablespoons oil over medium heat. When hot, add garlic, ginger, and lemongrass. Sauté for 1–2 minutes.
12. Add reserved fish flesh, paprika, chili powder, and turmeric. Stir and mash together until it resembles a paste. Decrease heat if necessary to avoid burning.
13. Add shrimp paste, fish sauce, blended pea puree, reserved poaching broth, and red onion.
14. Bring to a boil over high heat, then decrease the heat to a gentle simmer for about 20 minutes.
15. Taste and add salt as needed.
16. To assemble, rehydrate and strain noodles according to package instructions.
17. Prepare desired garnishes (boil eggs, slice limes, fry shallots, chop beans, clean and chop cilantro, and make pea crackers).
18. Divide noodles among six bowls, then ladle the soup broth over noodles, and lastly, add garnishes.

Maraq

Provided by Asho, ReWA Student

Variations of this simple, comforting, and nourishing stew are common in many countries in the Middle East, as well as Somalia. Asho enjoys making this dish for her young daughter. She often serves it with canjeero (see recipe, p. 40).

INGREDIENTS

2 tablespoons oil

½ onion, chopped

1 pound stew beef, cubed

3 tomatoes, chopped or ¾ cup canned
    diced tomatoes, drained

2 carrots, peeled and chopped
    (about 1 cup)

2 potatoes, peeled and chopped
    (about 1¾ cups)

2 cloves garlic, finely chopped

½ cup parsley, finely chopped

1 tablespoon ground cumin

1 teaspoon ground black pepper

1 tablespoon salt, divided

¾ teaspoon xawaash (optional,
    recipe, p. 14)

1 cup corn kernels (frozen is fine)

2 cups green beans, chopped
    into 1-inch pieces

1 cup okra (fresh or frozen),
    chopped (optional)

1 green pepper, thinly sliced

2 tablespoons finely chopped cilantro

1. Heat oil over medium-low in a large saucepan or stockpot. Add onion and sauté until translucent.
2. Increase heat to high. Add beef cubes and brown.
3. Add tomatoes and cook for 10 minutes over high heat, stirring occasionally.
4. Add carrots, potato, garlic, parsley, cumin, black pepper, salt, and xawaash if using, and cook on high for 5 minutes.
5. Add salt, corn, green beans, and okra, if using. Add water to cover. Simmer until meat and vegetables are tender, usually about an hour. Add green pepper and additional salt.
6. Garnish with cilantro and serve with rice or canjeero.

Yield: 6–8 side-dish servings

Shiro

Different versions provided by: Nigist Kidane, owner, Kezira Café; Kdsti, ReWA student; Afeworki Ghebreiyesus, family empowerment coordinator (pictured); Kibreab Ghebremariam, employment case manager.

Shiro is an East African comfort food, made clear by the fact that Nigist, Kdsti, Afeworki, and Kibreab *all* submitted recipes for this favorite. Naturally vegan and gluten-free, it is also nutritious and healthy. You can purchase chickpea powder at Ethiopian grocery stores. Most often you will find "mit'ten shiro" indicating that berbere and other ingredients are included. You will know that's what you have if the shiro has an orange hue.

INGREDIENTS

2 inches ginger, peeled and sliced

3 cups boiling water

1 yellow onion, peeled and roughly chopped

2 tablespoons canola oil

4 cloves garlic, minced

2 tablespoons fresh ginger, grated

1 tomato, diced

1 cup shiro (chickpea) powder

1 teaspoon salt

2 tablespoon niter kibbeh (recipe, p. 64)

Berbere, to taste (optional) (recipe, p. 58)

1. Place sliced ginger in boiling water, cover, and allow to steep for a minimum of 5 minutes. When ready to use, strain water through a colander into a bowl. Reserve the ginger water, and discard the ginger slices.
2. Place onion in a blender or food processor and whir until smooth.
3. Heat a heavy-bottomed pan over medium heat. Add onion puree along with 2 tablespoons ginger water and cook for 3 minutes, stirring frequently, so onions don't brown.
4. Add oil and cook for several minutes.
5. Add garlic, ginger, and berbere if using. Stir to combine. Add tomato and continue to cook for a few more minutes.
6. Mix shiro powder into the remaining ginger water and whisk thoroughly. Add to other ingredients. Add salt and niter kibbeh.
7. Cook on low for 30 minutes, stirring occasionally. Taste for seasoning and adjust.
8. Serve warm with injera.

KIBREAB

ReWA Employment Case Manager and Former ReWA Client • Eritrea

Kibreab was born in a big village in Eritrea. Before his life was changed so dramatically by the conflict in Eritrea, Kibreab received his bachelor's degree in plant science.

"I worked in several different positions in Eritrea and had a very comfortable life before political issues started to affect me. It became so bad that I was forced to cross the border into Sudan, risking my life. It was a perilous decision to make. Anybody can imagine how depressing and discouraging it was. Then I worked hard to leave for a secure and safe country, to find a better future."

After fleeing Eritrea, Kibreab was accepted into a master's degree program in China, where he completed his degree in plant breeding and genetics. He was a first-year PhD candidate there when he was assisted by the United Nations in a move to the US. Kibreab, his wife, and his son arrived in the US in 2015.

Since then the family has welcomed an American-born daughter, and Kibreab has gone from being a ReWA client to a ReWA employee.

"When I was new to the US, it was challenging to establish a life. Without the support of my case managers at the (IRC) and ReWA, I don't know what I would have done. My former ReWA employment case manager is now my colleague."

Yield: 6–8 servings

Zereshk Polo Morgh

Provided by Mahnaz Eshetu, ReWA executive director

This recipe is one of the most famous ones in Persian cuisine and is a celebration of food, meant to be shared at special gatherings. It is also known as "jeweled rice" because of the wild red barberries or *zereshk*, which contrast beautifully with the saffron hue of the rice and provide tartness. The recipe also calls for *baharat*, a mixture of spices that may include allspice, black pepper, cardamom, cassia bark, cloves, coriander, cumin, nutmeg, turmeric, saffron, ginger, paprika, and/or red chili pepper, commonly used in the Middle East and in Greece. It is available online and in specialty food markets. The spices and dried barberries can be found in Persian markets or online.

INGREDIENTS

4 cups long-grain basmati rice, rinsed

4 tablespoons salt, divided

1 teaspoon ground saffron

1 cup plus ¼ teaspoon sugar

½ teaspoon turmeric

¼ teaspoon sweet paprika

½ teaspoon baharat

¼ teaspoon pepper

2 garlic cloves, minced

1 tablespoon lemon juice

3 cups boiling water, divided

5 drops rose water

1 whole chicken, quartered

1 onion, sliced

7 tablespoons olive oil, divided

1 large potato, peeled and
   sliced in ⅛-inch rounds

4 tablespoons butter, divided

1 cup dried barberries, rinsed

2 tablespoons almond slivers, for garnish

2 tablespoons pistachios
   slivers, for garnish

1. Put rice and 3 tablespoons salt in bowl. Fill with water so that the rice is submerged. Soak for 1–2 hours.
2. Place 1 cup sugar in a small heat-proof bowl. Add 1 cup of boiling water. Stir until sugar dissolves into solution. Add dried barberries. Allow to soak while you prepare the rice.

3. Place saffron and ¼ teaspoon of sugar in mug, and add 1 cup boiling hot water. Stir until mixed and set aside for 10 minutes.

4. Combine turmeric, paprika, baharat, pepper and 1 teaspoon salt in a small bowl. Add the garlic, lemon juice, 1 cup hot water, and 1 tablespoon of saffron-sugar water. Stir well.

5. Preheat oven to 320°F. Line a deep baking pan with foil. Wash the chicken pieces, pat dry with a paper towel, and place on the pan. Lay onion over chicken and pour the spice-and-garlic mixture over the top. Cover with foil and bake for 1 hour.

6. Drain the soaking rice, add to a large, heavy-bottomed pot, and add 4 cups of water. Add 3 tablespoons of olive oil to stop the grains from sticking together. Cover the rice and boil for 10–15 minutes or until al dente. Drain in colander and pour into a bowl. Add 5 drops of rose water and 1 tablespoon saffron-sugar water to rice and mix well.

7. Put empty rice pot back on stove and add 4 tablespoons of oil. Lay the potato slices in the base of the pot. Top with the drained rice and cover with a lid. Cook on medium-high until the rice begins to steam. (Should take only a few minutes.)

8. Turn the heat to low, remove lid, wrap lid in a tea towel (covering the side facing the stove) and place back on the pot. The tea towel catches the condensation, preventing it from dripping back onto the rice. Leave to steam on low. Check after 45 minutes. May require 5 to 10 more minutes. Rice should be fluffy and separated when ready.

9. Drain barberries. Discard barberry sugar water. Heat 2 tablespoons butter in a frying pan and add the barberries. Sauté for a few minutes then add 2 tablespoons of sugar and 2 tablespoons of the saffron-sugar water. Stir briefly then remove from the heat.

10. Reserve 1 teaspoon of the saffron-sugar water. Reserve 1 cup of rice. Set both aside for step 12.

11. Place a layer of rice on a serving platter, followed by some of the barberries, nuts, and a little saffron-sugar water. Keep layering, mounding up into the shape of a cone. Leave some barberries and nuts for the top of the cone.

12. Melt the remaining butter and mix together in a bowl with the remaining saffron-sugar water. Mix in the final cup of rice.

13. Arrange the chicken quarters around the rice cone, then spoon the final cup of saffron-rice mixture and add it on top of the mound. Add a final sprinkling of barberries and nuts.

Mantu

Provided by Hila, ReWA Student

Mantu are Afghan dumplings, made with different types of meats and vegetables. Hila, a ReWA student, fills her mantu with ground beef, onions, cilantro, and spices. The dumplings are steamed, then served with a tangy yogurt, and topped with a spiced mixture of tomatoes, beans, and fresh mint leaves.

Hila was born and raised in Kunar, Afghanistan. She, her husband, and their five children miss their family in Afghanistan, but Hila feels much safer here, and she is particularly happy that she and her children are able to attend school.

INGREDIENTS

Dough

4 cups flour, plus ½ cup for rolling
1 teaspoon salt
2 eggs
1 tablespoon oil
¾ cup water

Filling

2 tablespoons oil
1 pound lean ground beef
2 cloves of garlic, minced
2 cups of onions, finely chopped
1½ teaspoons salt
1 teaspoon black pepper
2 teaspoons cumin
1 teaspoon turmeric
1½ teaspoons chili powder
1 cup cilantro, chopped

Topping

2 tablespoons oil, plus more for brushing
1 cup onion, chopped
2 cups fresh tomatoes, chopped, or
    1 (14-ounce) can diced tomatoes
1 clove garlic, minced
2 tablespoons green chili pepper,
    minced (optional)
1 teaspoon cumin
1 teaspoon paprika
½ teaspoon ground coriander
1 teaspoon salt
1 cup cooked kidney beans or
    1 (14-ounce) can, drained
¼ cup mint leaves, chopped, for garnish

Yogurt

2 cups plain Greek yogurt

2 tablespoons lemon juice

½ teaspoon salt

1. In a large bowl or stand mixer, combine the flour and salt together. Add oil and eggs and mix while adding water a little at a time until the ingredients combine. Knead with hands or a dough hook until the dough is firm and smooth. Cover with a damp towel or plastic wrap and let rest for at least 30 minutes.
2. In a pan, heat 2 tablespoons oil over medium heat and brown the meat. Add garlic and onion, and cook until translucent. Add salt, pepper, spices, and cilantro, and stir to mix well. Remove from the heat and place the contents of the pan in a heat-proof bowl. Let it cool for at least 10 minutes in the refrigerator.
3. On a flat, clean surface, sprinkle about ½ cup flour for rolling the dough.
4. Roll the dough into the shape of a log, and cut it into 3 parts. Use a rolling pin or pasta roller to flatten each part into a rectangular shape with a thickness of ⅛ inch.
5. Cut rolled dough into 3-inch squares. Use generous amounts of flour if the dough starts sticking.
6. Put about 1 teaspoon of the cooled meat mixture in the middle of each square, then fold the square into a pyramid by joining and pressing together opposing corners of the square. Seal the remaining corners and sides as you go. If the dough doesn't readily come together, wet the edges with your fingers to seal the dough. Continue this process with the other dough pieces. Store the dumplings on baking sheets lined with parchment, and cover them loosely with plastic wrap to prevent them from drying out.
7. Put an adequate amount of water in the bottom of a steamer pot and brush the bottom of the steamer pan with oil. Bring the water to a simmer. Put as many mantu as will comfortably fit into the steamer pan and steam for 6–7 minutes or until cooked through. Cook in batches if necessary.
8. While the dumplings are steaming, prepare the topping by heating the 2 tablespoons oil over medium heat in a frying pan. Sauté onion for 1–2 minutes. Add tomatoes, garlic, spices, and green chili, if desired. Lower heat to medium-low and cover. Cook for 5 minutes. Add beans and cook for another minute.
9. Mix yogurt base ingredients together and spread out on a large serving plate. Top with the mantu. Spoon the topping over the mantu and garnish with chopped mint. Serve immediately.

ABEBECH

ReWA Student • Ethiopia

Abebech grew up in Agagi, Ethiopia, where she lived with her mother and stepfather. She never knew her biological father, and her stepfather would beat her. At 16, she left for Sudan, where she had an auntie. She remembers crossing the border well. They drove to a rural area in Ethiopia, where they camped until they had enough people. Then the traffickers drove the group close to the border, where they dropped them off to walk across the border—through the River Bet. They took a boat across a large river, then crossed a smaller river by foot. She remembers the water being up to her neck.

It took several weeks of walking, driving, and camping—sleeping during the day and moving at night—before the group reached Khartoum, Sudan.

In Sudan, Abebech worked as a housekeeper and got married to a barber. Her family did not approve, and while her auntie eventually came around, her mother and stepfather disowned her and still have not visited her.

In Sudan, Abebech had her oldest child. However, they could not obtain citizenship in Sudan, so Abebech and her family left for Israel. The family lived in Israel for nine years. There, her husband continued working as a barber, and Abebech cooked in a restaurant, making Ethiopian food, including *kitfo*. Her youngest two children were born in Israel, but because they could not obtain citizenship there, they applied for refugee status in the US. In 2017, they were granted refugee status and moved to the US.

Since moving, Abebech has been learning English—she already speaks Eritrean, Arabic, Ahmaric, Hebrew, and Oromo—and attends classes at ReWA. She is already anticipating the day she can apply for US citizenship. She is very happy to be in the US because she finally feels like she has freedom.

Yield: 6 servings

Kitfo

Provided by Abebech, ReWA Student

The East African version of steak tartar, kitfo is considered a delicacy by ReWA's Ethiopian and Eritrean students. Though sometimes the meat is kept raw, Abebech decided to share this slightly cooked version.

Don't buy packaged ground beef for this dish. Instead, visit your butcher and tell them exactly what the meat is for, and have them grind it for you. *Mitmita*, a fiery spice blend, and seven-spice mix can both be purchased in East African groceries or online. Kitfo is often served with Ethiopian cheese, ayib (see recipe, p. 33), and injera (see recipe, p. 32).

INGREDIENTS

2 pounds beef for kitfo
4 teaspoons mitmita
1 teaspoon berbere (recipe, p. 58)
1½ teaspoons seven-spice mix
½ teaspoon salt
1 teaspoon black pepper
3 cloves garlic, peeled and ground
½-inch ginger, peeled and ground

¼ teaspoon vegetable oil
1 small yellow onion, peeled
    and finely chopped
4 tablespoons niter kibbeh
    (recipe, p. 64), divided
1 green bell pepper, stemmed,
    seeded, and diced

1. Add beef, mitmita, berbere, seven-spice mix, salt, pepper, garlic, ginger, and oil in a deep bowl. Mix well by hand, wearing sterile gloves if you like.
2. Select a pan that retains heat, like a heavy cast-iron pan. Heat over medium.
3. Add chopped onions to the dry pan, stirring occasionally until brown.
4. Combine the meat mixture with the onions in the pan. Mix 1 tablespoon of niter kibbeh into the meat using a long-handled fork or spoon. Add a second tablespoon of the niter kibbeh. Repeat the process, 1 tablespoon at a time. As soon as all the butter is incorporated into the meat mixture, remove the pan from the heat. Transfer the kitfo to a serving dish.
5. Add diced green bell pepper, mix, and serve.

Yield: 6 servings

Misir Wot

Provided by Nigist Kidane, Owner of Kezira Café in Seattle

Eritrea was colonized by Italy, and its cuisine and cooking methods were influenced greatly by Italian foods. Nigist says she sees parallels between Italian dishes and the flavorful misir wot, a red lentil stew. The amount of oil versus water that a cook chooses to use in East African dishes varies. Nigist notes that Eritrean cooks tend to use less oil than Ethiopian cooks.

INGREDIENTS

2 inches ginger, peeled and sliced

1 yellow onion, minced

1 tablespoon canola oil

4 cloves garlic, minced

2 inches fresh ginger, peeled and grated (about 2 tablespoons)

3–4 tablespoons berbere (recipe, p. 58)

2 tomatoes, cored and diced

1½ teaspoons salt

2 cups red lentils, washed and drained

1 teaspoon ground cardamom

1. Bring 4 cups of water to a boil in a small pot and turn off the heat. Place sliced ginger in the boiled water. Allow to steep for at least 5 minutes. Strain and reserve water, discarding the ginger slices.

2. Place a medium-sized pot on medium heat. Add onion and 2 tablespoons water. Gently sauté the onions with water until just translucent, for about 3 minutes. Do not brown the onions.

3. Add oil, garlic, grated ginger, berbere, and salt. Fry for several more minutes. Add tomato, 2 cups ginger water, red lentils, and cardamom. Cover the pot. Simmer on medium-low heat for 30–45 minutes or until the lentils are soft, stirring regularly. To avoid scorching, periodically add more ginger water while stirring. You will likely use 4 or more cups of ginger water before the misir wot is done.

Yield: 6 servings

Kik Wot

Provided by Nigist Kidane, owner of Kezira Café in Seattle

Nigest's kik wot is similar to misir wot, but trades spice and heat for the more familiar flavors of ginger and garlic. The turmeric-spiked yellow lentils look striking served alongside misir wot or on injera (pictured, p. 63).

INGREDIENTS

1-inch ginger, peeled and sliced
1 yellow onion, minced
1¼ tablespoons canola oil
4 cloves garlic, minced

2 inches fresh ginger, peeled and
    grated (about 2 tablespoons)
2 tablespoons turmeric powder
1½ teaspoons salt
2 cups yellow split peas

1. Wash the split peas multiple times in cold, fresh water. Drain the water and repeat until the water runs clear. Drain one last time and set aside.
2. Bring 4 cups of water to a boil and add sliced ginger. Remove from the heat, cover with a lid, and allow the ginger to steep for at least 5 minutes.
3. Strain water through colander to remove ginger slices. Reserve the water and discard the ginger slices.
4. Place a heavy-bottomed pot over medium heat. Add onion and 2 tablespoons of the ginger water and sauté for about 3 minutes until the onion is just translucent. Add oil, garlic, ginger, turmeric, and salt. Fry for 5 more minutes while stirring continuously.
5. Add remaining water and split peas. Cover the pot. Simmer on low heat for 30–45 minutes or until soft, stirring regularly. Do not allow the bottom to scorch.

AHMAD

ReWA SeaTac ESL Student • Eritrea

Ahmad originally hails from a pastoral area in Eritrea, where his family farmed wheat and other crops, raised goats and cows for meat and milk, and kept bees for honey. When he was older, Ahmad became a fisherman in his country. Ahmad came to the US in 2012, like so many others fleeing the war between Eritrea and Ethiopia. He misses the food and people of his country, and, of course, his family. Over time, he has come to think of the US as his home, but he hopes to visit Eritrea once he becomes a US citizen. Ahmad is very happy the war between Eritrea and Ethiopia is finally over, but he knows it will be many years before the economy and infrastructure of his country will be repaired.

Yield: 8–12 servings

Barbecued Goat

Provided by Ahmad, ReWA Student

In his native Eritrea, Ahmad celebrated special occasions outdoors by grilling goat or beef in this fashion, a technique he learned from his father-in-law. Ahmad prefers to enjoy the heady aromas and smoky flavors of the freshly cooked meat without side dishes. In his home country, Ahmad would need to slaughter the goat by slitting its throat with a sharp knife, then bleed it, skin it, and clean it himself. In the US, you can order a cleaned, dressed goat from a halal or specialty butcher.

INGREDIENTS

1 18–20-pound kid goat, cleaned   Salt
   and dressed, cut into pieces   Pepper

1. Build a hot fire roughly 3 feet in diameter, using wood or a combination of wood and charcoal. Or, use a charcoal grill.
2. Place a metal grill over the fire.
3. When the fire has burned down, spread embers so that the thickest cuts are over the hotter part of the fire, while the thinner and smaller cuts cook over the embers.
4. Season the meat with salt and pepper.
5. Roast the goat, turning often, until done, roughly 40 minutes.
6. Remove from heat, cover, and allow meat to rest for 10–15 minutes. Serve warm.

EYEPAW

SeaTac ESL Student • Burma

Eyepaw is from a small city in Burma. Although Eyepaw's family is Buddhist, she converted to Christianity when she married her husband, a rice farmer. As part of the Christian minority, Eyepaw and her husband were persecuted and forced to flee to a refugee camp in Thailand. Thousands of Kachin and Chin people had been attacked with artillery, helicopter guns, and infantry in Burma. Eyepaw and her husband resided in Thailand for about 17 years, and sold the Burmese dishes that Eyepaw cooked for a living. One of the dishes is *nga baung doke*—the recipe that she shares in this book.

The couple's five children were all born in Thailand, and although they liked it there, Eyepaw's husband wanted their children to be educated, which led to their immigration to the US in 2013. Sadly, Eyepaw's husband died of lung cancer three years ago—a loss that Eyepaw feels deeply.

Eyepaw uses her culinary skills to make sandwiches and salads at Alki bakery. She's proud of her work there and enjoys spending time with her Burmese colleagues— they often share traditional meals at work and celebrate holidays as a community.

Eyepaw's family is scattered—her mother remains in Burma, her father and sister are in Thailand, and her brother is in Arizona. Eyepaw sends some of the money she earns back home to her mother in Burma. She misses her family, especially her late, beloved husband, with whom she experienced so much. But she appreciates Seattle for its beauty and proximity to the water. In the summer, she loves to swim every day.

Yield: About a dozen parcels

Nga Baung Doke

Provided by Eyepaw, ReWA Student

This classic Burmese dish is most often made with fish, but Eyepaw's preferred version features loads of interesting vegetables steamed in banana leaves. You can find frozen banana leaves in many Asian grocery stores and markets, or you can use aluminum foil as a substitute, but you will of course miss out on the delicate flavor imparted by banana leaves. This is one of the dishes that Eyepaw sold in the market to make a living during her time in Thailand.

INGREDIENTS

3 packages of banana leaves, thawed

2 cloves garlic, minced

1 tablespoon fresh ginger, finely minced

12 small Thai red chili peppers, finely chopped

2 sticks lemongrass, bruised and finely chopped

1 large onion, sliced thinly lengthwise

3 shallots, sliced thinly lengthwise

4 cups mushrooms (such as shitake, cremini, or oyster), cleaned, stemmed, and sliced into strips

4 cups bean sprouts

2 chayote squash, sliced into 2-inch matchsticks

1 (20-ounce) can of bamboo shoots, drained and sliced into strips

2 tablespoons salt

2 tablespoons Knorr granulated chicken bouillon (omit for vegetarian version)

½ cup vegetable oil

1¼ teaspoons ground turmeric

⅓ cup fish sauce (omit for vegetarian version)

1 (14-ounce) package of rice flour

Round toothpicks

Sharp scissors

Large pot with steam basket or steaming tower

1. Wipe banana leaves clean with a damp cloth. Using sharp scissors, cut into footlong sections and set aside.
2. In a mortar and pestle, grind garlic, ginger, chilis, and lemongrass into a paste. Alternatively, this can be done on a cutting board with the bottom of a heavy mug or bowl.

3. In a large bowl, combine the rest of the ingredients. Mix well with your hands (you may want to wear gloves).
4. Add the spice paste and mix until thoroughly incorporated.
5. Mixture should be moist. If not, add water about ½ cup at a time until the mixture is wet, but not watery.
6. Layer 2–3 sheets of banana leaves and place about 1 cup of the mixture in the middle.
7. Fold in all sides to form a parcel, and secure with a toothpick about an inch above the mixture. With scissors, trim the excess leaves an inch above the toothpick straight across the parcel.
8. In a large pot fitted with a steam basket or the base of a steamer tower, bring about 4 cups of water to a boil.
9. Place parcels in a steamer basket or on a tray with the toothpick side up, and steam for 20–30 minutes. Check the water level periodically to avoid scorching the bottom of the pot. Steam in batches if necessary.
10. Serve warm on the banana leaves accompanied by white rice.

Yield: 4 servings

Nan Gyi Thoke

Provided by Ni Ni, ReWA Student

This tasty curried noodle salad offered by Ni Ni is a Burmese classic that is served for breakfast, lunch, or as a snack. It is light, yet satisfying, hitting all the right notes: sweet, salty, sour, umami, and bitter. Like many Burmese dishes, this one can be customized to your liking with an array of condiments to add heat, herbal notes, and crunch.

INGREDIENTS

6 tablespoons oil

6 shallots, finely chopped

5 cloves garlic, minced

1 teaspoon turmeric powder

2 teaspoons chili powder

4 boneless skinless chicken breasts, thinly sliced (substitute tofu if desired)

2 teaspoons salt

2 teaspoons fish sauce

2 cups water

16 ounces rice noodles

Hard-boiled eggs, quartered

Garlic chili oil

Fish sauce

Chili flakes

Chickpea powder, toasted

Bean sprouts

Shredded cabbage

Sliced red onion

Cilantro

Puffed rice noodles (fry rice noodles)

Limes, cut in wedges

1. Heat the oil in a large skillet over medium-low heat. Add shallot and garlic and sauté until fragrant. Add turmeric and sauté for another minute or so.
2. Add chili powder and chicken and stir. Add water and bring to a boil. Add salt and fish sauce, and lower the heat to a simmer.
3. While chicken is simmering, prepare rice noodles according to package directions.
4. To serve, put a handful of noodles in a bowl and add a few spoonfuls of the sauce and chicken. Garnish with egg, garlic chili oil, a sprinkle of chickpea powder, a few drops of fish sauce, a shake of chili flakes, and a handful each of bean sprouts, cabbage, red onion, cilantro, and puffed rice noodles. Serve with a lime wedge.

Yield: Serves a crowd

Lamb Kabsa

Provided by Najwa, ReWA Student

Since arriving in Seattle as refugees in 2014, Najwa and her husband, Fawaz, have opened a catering business specializing in Middle Eastern food. The couple is thrilled to be able to provide for the needs of their five young children with the income they make in their new business. While they are grateful for their financial successes, nothing makes them prouder than the way their children transitioned to life in the US so quickly. Within a few short months of arriving, their eldest daughter had learned English and made new friends.

Najwa is happy that ReWA celebrates quarterly graduation parties with class potlucks. She shared this delicious *lamb kabsa* with her teachers and other students in the ReWA ESL program at one of the celebrations. This recipe makes a lot! Try preparing it for your next large party or gathering.

This recipe includes dried limes, which can be purchased at Middle Eastern grocery stores or online. These limes have been boiled in salt brine and left to dry in the sun. The taste is similar to sumac—kind of like a complex super citrus. Piercing them allows their flavor to infuse the dish, lending a pleasingly sour and bright flavor.

INGREDIENTS

5½ pounds of bone-in lamb,
    cut into large cubes

Rice

3 cups basmati rice
2 tablespoons butter
2¼ pounds onion, finely chopped
6–8 garlic cloves, minced
1 green bell pepper, seeded
    and finely diced
1 pinch ground cumin
1 pinch ground coriander

¼ teaspoon ground green cardamom
½ teaspoon ground cinnamon
½ teaspoon ground allspice
¼ teaspoon white pepper
½ teaspoon ground dried lime powder
Salt
Ground black pepper
2¼ pounds tomatoes, peeled and diced

Sauce

2 tablespoons butter
1 large onion, finely chopped

3 garlic cloves, minced

1 cup chopped tomatoes

10 whole dried limes, pierced

1 tablespoon tomato paste

¼ cup diced celery

¼ teaspoon cinnamon

Salt

2 cups water

Garnish

¼ cup toasted pine nuts

Rice

1. In a heavy pot set over high heat, sear lamb until brown on all sides. Add enough water to the pot so that the water level is 2 inches above the meat. Bring to a boil and then cook gently over medium heat for 1½–2 hours or until tender. Strain meat, reserve stock, and set meat aside. Cover it to keep warm.
2. Wash rice, drain water, and then refill the bowl with water. Soak for 15 minutes. Drain, rinse under running water, and then drain again.
3. Add butter to a large stock pot or casserole. Over medium heat, add onion, garlic, green bell pepper, cumin, coriander, cardamom, cinnamon, allspice, white pepper, ground dried lime powder, salt, and black pepper, and fry until the onion is translucent. Add peeled tomatoes. Reduce the heat to low and cook for about 10 minutes, or until tender.
4. Add rice to vegetables in the pot. Cook over medium heat for 5 minutes.
5. Pour meat stock into the pot until it is approximately 1½ inches above the rice. Cover the pot and cook on low heat for 30 minutes or until the rice is tender. Check and stir periodically. Add more stock or water if the rice begins to look dry and to prevent scorching on the bottom.

Sauce

1. Make the sauce in a medium-sized sauté pan. Heat 2 tablespoons butter over medium heat until foam appears, and then add onion, garlic, and tomato. Fry until the onion becomes soft. Add dried limes, tomato paste, celery, cinnamon, salt, and water. Cook until the mixture is slightly thickened and the celery becomes tender. Add sauce to the rice. Mix well.
2. On a large platter, layer a bed of rice, top with meat, and garnish with pine nuts.

LOI

ReWA Staff • Vietnam

Loi's family loves her food. Once when her son was on a diet, she cooked chicken rice and her son ate and ate until he had to tell her to stop making it so that he could go back on his diet. When she brings her food to potlucks, everyone asks for her recipes.

Loi comes from Phan Thiet, Vietnam. She remembers her mother and father as very gentle and humane people. They often fed and accommodated the homeless in their town, even going without food themselves to feed others. Loi's mother had high aspirations for her children, with plans for a strong education and a good future for them. Tragically, Loi's mother died when her brother was only six and Loi was just twenty-one months old. "My brother and I were the happiest children in our village, and in just a short time we became the most unfortunate children. We lost a very great mother."

Loi learned to be resourceful in her early years. At eight, she taught herself how to knit by copying an elderly woman and using incense sticks and fishing net. When her father saw how much she liked knitting, he made her a pair of bamboo needles. Loi would save her breakfast money to buy yarn and she began knitting passionately.

At age eighteen, Loi met her husband and they went on to have five children. Because her husband was an officer for the South Vietnamese army, after the war he was imprisoned in a reeducation camp for six and a half years. During this time, Loi struggled to raise her family and make ends meet—no one would hire family members of South Vietnamese officers. But Loi still managed to save enough money by selling tea to purchase a small house. She was also able to send her children to school.

After Loi's husband's release, the US government sponsored Loi and her family's move to Seattle in 1995. In 1997, Loi was going to college full time and taking care of her whole family. She had to cook three meals a day, go to class, do chores, and would finish her homework at 2:30 a.m. While in school, Loi received an honors award.

Although Loi misses her native land, she likes living in Seattle. She is very grateful for her family, especially her youngest son, who takes care of her in her old age. She deeply misses her middle son, who passed away. Today, she works at ReWA doing food outreach and translation work. She considers ReWA to be her family and is excited to see it growing.

Yield: 4 servings

Mixed Fried Rice

Provided by Loi Ho, ReWA Basic Food Case Manager and Senior Meal Lead

As a mother of five and a grandmother of six, Loi has had many years to perfect her fried-rice recipe. Loi's grandchildren say of fried rice made by anyone else, "but it's not as good as *Bā Nôi's*!" (Bā Nôi, pronounced *Baa Noy*, means grandmother in Vietnamese.)

INGREDIENTS

2 cups long-grain rice

3 eggs

½ teaspoon salt

¾ teaspoon black pepper

1 tablespoon and 2 teaspoons
    olive oil, divided

4 cloves garlic, minced

4 green onions, sliced

1 carrot, diced

5 ounces green beans, cut
    into ⅛-inch lengths

6 ounces mushrooms, diced

3 tablespoons soy sauce, divided

12 fresh prawns, peeled and deveined

8 ounces cured sausage (pork, turkey,
    or chicken), sliced in thin rounds

1. Cook rice in advance, but reduce water by one-quarter the amount you would normally use. Allow to cool to room temperature.
2. Heat 2 teaspoons oil in wok or wide pan over medium heat. Crack eggs into bowl and whisk. Add a pinch each of the salt and pepper. Pour egg into the pan and cook as if making an omelet, lifting the edges to allow uncooked egg to run underneath. Remove from pan and cut into narrow strips. Set aside.
3. Heat 1 tablespoon oil in wok until nearly smoking. Add garlic and green onions, and fry for 2 minutes.
4. Add carrot, green beans, mushrooms, and half of the soy sauce. Fry for 5 minutes.
5. Add prawns, sausages, and the remaining soy sauce, salt, and pepper; toss to combine.
6. Add rice and mix. Using a flat turner, spatula, or large spoon, press down on the rice firmly. Allow rice mixture to fry, without stirring, for 2 minutes. Repeat this process 6 times, for a total of 12 minutes.
7. Add eggs, mix well with the rice, and serve.

Yield: 4–6 servings

Zigni

Beef version provided by Kdsti, ReWA Student. Lamb version provided by Zerai, ReWA Student.

Eritrean cuisine is full of spicy meat stews like this one, usually served with injera. While Kdsti prepares her version of *zigni* using beef, Zerai, a fellow student, prefers lamb. Try both versions!

INGREDIENTS

2 pounds beef or lamb, cubed

3 small red onions, peeled
  and finely chopped

3 cloves garlic, minced

½ cup vegetable oil, plus 2 tablespoons

¼ teaspoon salt, plus more to season meat

3–4 tablespoons berbere (recipe, p. 58)

1 teaspoon grated fresh ginger

2 tablespoons tomato paste

2 large tomatoes, diced

1–2 teaspoons chopped fresh rosemary

1. Season the meat with salt and pepper. Place a large lidded pot over medium-high heat and brown the meat, in batches if necessary. Remove from the pan and set aside.
2. Add onions, garlic, and 2 tablespoons vegetable oil to the pot used to brown the meat. Cook on medium-low heat while stirring often. Cover and cook for about 15 minutes. Use more oil as needed.
3. After the onions have cooked, add berbere, tomato paste, and ¼ teaspoon salt and stir until combined. Add ½ cup oil. Cook the mixture for a few minutes, then add fresh tomatoes. Turn the heat to medium and stir often to cook the tomatoes.
4. Add 2 cups water to the onion-and-tomato mixture and bring to a boil. Reduce the heat and simmer. Keep covered for 30 minutes.
5. Add meat and rosemary to the pan and simmer; keep covered for additional 30 minutes. Remove lid if needed to allow the moisture to evaporate and the mixture to thicken.

Adobo

Provided by Sarah Aranez, ReWA Housing Coordinator for Homelessness Prevention Program

There are as many variations on adobo as there are Filipino mothers around the world. These are Sarah's two favorites—one with pork and one with chicken, both served with rice. While they are the same dish, Sarah says that the different densities and flavors of the meats require their own process. For example, while it would be fine to marinate the pork for up to 24 hours, the chicken would become very salty if left in this marinade for that long. It is not simply a matter of using the same recipe and subbing in a different protein. Toasted garlic can be purchased in most grocery stores—or you can gently fry thinly sliced garlic until light brown.

INGREDIENTS

Chicken Adobo

4 pounds of bone-in chicken thighs, legs, and/or wings

½ cup of soy sauce

¼ cup white vinegar or apple cider vinegar

½ tablespoon ground black pepper

3 tablespoons garlic, minced

½ tablespoons brown sugar, adjust and balance sourness and sweetness

4 dried bay leaves

¼ cup mild vegetable oil

Fresh jalapeño peppers or Thai chilis, stemmed and minced (optional)

Toasted garlic, for garnish

1. Place chicken in a large glass dish. In a medium bowl, whisk together soy sauce, vinegar, pepper, fresh garlic, brown sugar, and bay leaves. Pour the marinade over the chicken and marinate for about 1 hour.
2. Place chicken and marinade into a pot. Cover the pot and place it over medium heat. When the contents start to simmer, turn the heat to low. Stir occasionally, always replacing the cover after, and simmer for 20 minutes.

3. Add oil and fresh peppers or chilis, if using. Replace the lid and simmer for 20–40 minutes longer, stirring occasionally or until the sauce becomes thick.
4. Garnish with toasted garlic.

Pork Adobo

2 pounds pork belly, cut into 2-inch cubes	5 bay leaves
2 tablespoons minced garlic	1 tablespoon whole peppercorns
½ cup soy sauce	2 cups water
4 tablespoons white vinegar	Salt

1. Place the pork in a glass dish or any other nonreactive dish. Add soy sauce and garlic, and toss to coat. Cover and refrigerate for a minimum of 1 hour, but no more than 24 hours.
2. Heat a heavy pot on medium. Drain the pork of any liquid, and sear the pork belly in batches until all pieces are brown, approximately for 2–3 minutes. Individual pieces of pork should not crowd each other during the searing process.
3. Return all seared pork to pot. Add vinegar. Bring to a boil for 5 minutes.
4. Add bay leaves, peppercorns, and water, and then return to a boil. Lower heat and cover. Simmer for 40–50 minutes or until the pork belly is soft and the sauce has thickened.
5. Add salt.

SOOKJAI

Current ReWA Staff Member • Thailand

I n Thailand, Sookjai worked as a training manager and project director for the Peace Corps. She married an American citizen, whom she had met on a trip to Seattle. When her husband became ill, the couple moved to Seattle, where Sookjai's husband could get a kidney transplant.

In Seattle, both Sookjai and her husband worked for ReWA—Sookjai as a Thai-Lao advocate. It's been Sookjai's only job in the US. Her husband died in 2011 of skin cancer related to low immunity. Since then, Sookjai has remarried. She has no kids, but she does have a treasured cat named Frisco. She values her work at ReWA. "Without ReWA I wouldn't have the ability to help."

Yield: 6 servings

Golden Triangle Chicken Curry

Provided by Sookjai Bashore, ReWA Thai and Lao Domestic Violence Survivor's Advocate

Sookjai is Thai, but the Golden Triangle referenced in her curry's name is the region of Southeast Asia where the borders of Thailand, Laos, and Burma meet. Just as the three cultures have greatly influenced each other due to their close proximity, their cuisines share some similarities, as well. The spices and roots in Sookjai's curry cross international borders in that geographic region.

INGREDIENTS

Curry Paste
2 teaspoons coriander seeds
¼ teaspoon cumin seeds
3 stalks of lemongrass, white parts only
5 red Thai chilis
1 chile negro chili, soaked in hot
  water to soften (can be found
  in Mexican markets)
1 3-inch piece of fresh turmeric, peeled
3 small (or 1 large) shallots
5 cloves garlic, peeled
1 2-inch piece of ginger, peeled
7⅛-inch-thick slices of galangal
½ teaspoon black peppercorns

Curry
2 tablespoons mild vegetable oil
2 tablespoons curry paste
1 (16-ounce) can coconut
  milk, stirred, divided
3 boneless, skinless chicken breasts,
  cut into long, slim slices
4 cups chicken stock
16 ounces sliced bamboo shoots,
  vacuum-sealed or canned, drained
3 bell peppers, cut in long ½-inch slices
5–10 fresh Thai lime leaves
2 cups fresh Thai basil
Fish sauce (optional)
Fresh Thai chili, sliced (optional)
Salt

1. In dry pan, roast coriander and cumin seeds on low heat for 2 minutes. Add seeds and all remaining curry paste ingredients into a food processor or a blender jar. Process to make a finely ground paste.

2. Heat vegetable oil in a heavy-bottomed pot over medium heat. Add 2 tablespoons curry paste and sauté for 1–2 minutes, or until fragrant. Add ½ can of coconut milk. When the contents begin to simmer, add chicken. Simmer for 2 more minutes.
3. Add remaining coconut milk and chicken stock. Bring back to a simmer and add bamboo shoots and bell pepper. Continue to simmer for 20 minutes longer. Add salt.
4. Add lime leaves and remove from the heat after 2 minutes.
5. Garnish with basil and season with fish sauce, Thai chili, or both.

SAYED

ReWA Staff • Afghanistan

Sayed is originally from Parwan province, but he grew up in Kabul. He worked for the US Embassy, first as an interpreter, and then as an assistant manager for subcontractors. Anyone working with the US lived under the danger of violence and murder. People who have worked with the US Armed Forces or under the Chief of Mission Authority in Afghanistan and Iraq qualify for special immigrant visas. To qualify for this status, applicants must detail the threats they and their families experienced and received. It was through this program that Sayed, his wife, and their child were able to immigrate to Seattle, where he now works as a case worker for ReWA.

Sayed explained that the decision to move to the US was for security, job opportunities, education, and a good economy. However, it was a difficult decision because they had to leave so many family members behind. For Sayed and his family, the choice was clear despite missing so many loved ones. They arrived in Seattle in October 2016.

Sayed has learned that it is difficult even for educated immigrants to land good jobs in the US—especially because credentials don't always transfer. Sayed started at entry-level jobs, took classes, and eventually worked his way to a job as an interpreter at ReWA in 2018. His advice for other immigrants: "Go to school, college, university to lead a better life. Otherwise life will always be a struggle. Education is the only way to make a difference for yourself and your family."

Yield: 8–10 servings

Kebab

Provided by Sayed Sadat, ReWA Staff

According to Sayed, these kebabs are both delicious and famous in his native country, Afghanistan, where they are usually grilled on metal skewers. Because many people cannot afford to eat meat every day, kebabs are considered a special-occasion food. Available from your butcher, the addition of lamb fat adds mouth-watering flavor and ensures that the lamb stays moist. Some recipes include yogurt, cumin, coriander, and/or other spices in the marinade, but Sayed prefers to let the flavor of the lamb shine through. You can use a gas grill, but you won't be able to achieve the characteristic smoky flavor.

INGREDIENTS

4 pounds boneless lamb leg, cut
    into 1½-inch–2 inch cubes
1 pound lamb fat, cut into small pieces
    (or 4 tablespoons neutral oil)
2 onions, peeled, chopped, and
    pureed with a bit of water

1 whole head of garlic, peeled and
    finely grated or chopped
2 teaspoons salt
2 teaspoons ground black pepper
2 teaspoons cayenne (optional)
Chopped green chili and tomato (optional)

1. Combine onion puree, garlic, salt, and pepper.
2. Mix lamb, and fat if using, with the marinade. Cover and refrigerate for at least 5–6 hours, preferably overnight.
3. If using wooden skewers, soak them in warm water to prevent them from burning.
4. Alternate the lamb, fat pieces, tomatoes, and green chilis, if using, on the skewers. If not using fat, brush the kebabs with oil.
5. Build the fire and allow it to burn down to hot coals. Place grill 3–4 inches above heat.
6. Grill skewers for about 10 minutes and turn over at the halfway point.
7. Sprinkle with additional salt, black pepper, and cayenne if desired. Serve warm with green pepper, tomato, and naan.

HASSINA

SeaTac ESL Student • Afghanistan

Hassina is from Kabul, Afghanistan. She arrived in Seattle with her husband and five children in February 2018. Both her husband and her father-in-law were chefs in their country. Her husband worked as a chef in a nice restaurant in Kabul, but there was no life for them there as it was not safe.

Today, her husband cooks at Starbucks, a job he likes. Hassina is also happy to be in Seattle. She is so busy raising her small children and taking English classes at ReWA that she sometimes doesn't even have time to eat breakfast. Fortunately, her husband helps with cooking at home when he can.

Yield: 6–8 servings

Qabli

This version was provided by Hassina, ReWA Student. Reza Sakhi, ReWA Post-Secondary Success Coach, provided a similar version.

This delectable rice dish with carrots, almonds, and raisins is the national dish of Afghanistan. No gathering or celebration would be complete without the warmly spiced and flavorful *qabli*, so much so that different variations on this recipe were submitted by not one but two people from the ReWA community. Reza's favorite qabli features lamb, which is the most common preparation, but beef or chicken can be used as substitutes. You can also omit meat from the recipe, or replace it with another protein, to make this vegetarian, as Hassina often does for ReWA ESL-class potlucks. This recipe is tradition-ally made with Afghan Golden Sella basmati rice, a type of presteamed basmati, but reg-ular basmati rice will also work. The important thing is that the rice grains should remain separate and distinct for a fluffy *pilaf.* Hassina's husband was a chef in a fine restaurant in Kabul, so he helps her prepare this dish at home. Different flavor variations are achieved through cardamom, cinnamon, cumin, saffron, and pistachios.

Reza describes his mother as a "very professional cook," even though she did not cook outside of his family home. Today, Reza's wife, who is also Afghani, makes this dish in Seattle. He says his wife's version is very good, but it is not the same dish that his mother used to make, probably due to the ingredients not being available in the US.

INGREDIENTS

3 cups Golden Sella or regular basmati rice
¼ cup vegetable oil
2 pounds lamb, chicken, or beef, cubed
1 large yellow onion, diced
2 teaspoons salt
1 teaspoon black pepper

1–3 teaspoons garam masala
1 cup raisins (Hassina prefers
   dried Red Flame)
3 carrots, peeled and cut into matchsticks
½ cup slivered almonds, lightly toasted
3 cups hot water

1. Soak the rice in cold water for 20–30 minutes (2 hours if using Golden Sella rice). Rinse 2–3 times to remove the starch, and drain.

2. Heat oil over medium heat in a large, heavy-bottomed pan. Season meat with salt and pepper, and brown on all sides. Remove from the pan and set aside.

3. Add onions to the pan in which you browned the meat, and sauté until it is translucent and starts to brown. Add 2 teaspoons salt, 1 teaspoon pepper, and garam masala, and stir for 1–2 minutes.

4. Transfer the meat back to the pan and add water. Simmer for about 1½ hours until the meat is fork tender.

5. Add rice and stir gently. Add raisins, carrots, and almonds. Cover with a tight-fitting lid and simmer for about 20 minutes.

6. Remove from the heat and let it rest for 10 minutes before serving with the lid on. Traditionally, the rice is served mounded over the meat. Add a sprinkling of garam masala on top.

MARGARITA

ReWA Finance Director • Venezuela, Spain, Hungary

Margarita has served as ReWA's finance director since 2017 and is bilingual in Spanish and English. She was born in Venezuela and now watches the current events in that country with a heavy heart. Margarita was a very young child when her family moved to the US. She does not have memories of living in her birthplace, but she recalls her father lamenting the chaos within the Venezuelan government and bureaucracy. Margarita's Spanish mother and Hungarian father left their homelands for Venezuela at a time when that country had a democratic government and a strong economy. These advantages beckoned to them, signaling opportunity and hope. Sadly, Venezuela is a mere shadow of the country it was when her family lived there. Throughout her life, Margarita's father talked about the mounting social and economic pressures that led to the family leaving the country. It is a reminder of how a rich, beautiful country can deteriorate when democracy is lost.

Yield: 4–6 servings

Goulash and Dumplings

Provided by Margarita Seeley, ReWA Finance Director

This paprika-spiced stew hails from Hungary, the birth country of Margarita's father. A dish with a rich history that originated with the herders, goulash is made with tougher, less expensive cuts of meat. The long cooking time makes the meat tender and thickens the stew as well.

INGREDIENTS

Goulash
2 tablespoons olive oil
2 yellow onions, minced
2 pounds beef, cubed
Salt and pepper
3 tablespoons tomato paste
3 tablespoons sweet paprika

2 cups beef stock
⅓ cup of sour cream

Dumplings
1 cup all-purpose flour
1 egg
¼ cup water
¼ teaspoon salt

1. To make the goulash, add olive oil to a large pot set over medium heat. Add onion and cook until translucent.
2. Add beef and cook until it is brown, without burning the onion. Add salt and pepper.
3. Add tomato paste, paprika, and beef stock. Bring to a simmer, cover, and cook over low heat for about 2 hours, or until the meat is tender, stirring occasionally.
4. Combine all dumpling ingredients together and knead for 5 minutes. Cover with a dishtowel and let the dough rest for 45 minutes.
5. Twenty minutes before the goulash is done cooking, take a tablespoon of dough with one spoon and use a second spoon to scoop the dough out into the goulash.
6. Add more salt if needed. Cover and cook for 20 minutes until the dumplings are cooked through.
7. Remove from the heat and add sour cream. Stir until creamy.

Yield: 6 servings

Caldo Gallego

Provided by Margarita Seeley, ReWA Finance Director

Margarita considers several countries *home*. She was born in Venezuela, her mother is from Spain, and her father is from Hungary. The whole family emigrated from Venezuela to the US when Margarita was very young. Her mother returned to live in Spain after retirement, and Margarita regularly cooks Spanish cuisine, making the distance between them just a little bit shorter. For Margarita, *caldo gallego*, a hearty white bean soup, is one Spanish dish that conjures up memories of her mother. Look for Spanish chorizo, a paprika-spiced cured sausage. Don't use Mexican chorizo, which is sold fresh and spiced with cumin and chilis. Ideally, this soup is served with crusty bread and is even better the following day, after the flavors have had a chance to meld.

INGREDIENTS

12 ounces dried white beans (canned beans can be used as a substitute)

½-pound piece beef chuck steak

3 slices of bacon, cut into bite-size pieces

3 tablespoons olive oil, divided

8 ounces Spanish chorizo (kielbasa can be used as a substitute)

1 onion, minced

6 cloves garlic, thinly sliced

3 quarts chicken stock or water

1 pork hock or ham bone

2 bay leaves

4 white medium potatoes, scrubbed and diced into bite-size pieces

1 turnip, peeled and diced into bite-size pieces

2 cups (packed) cabbage, collard greens, or kale, without stems, shredded

Salt

Pepper

If using dried beans, put the beans in a heavy pot and cover with 3 inches of water the day before cooking. Soak beans overnight. While it's not necessary to soak them longer than 8 hours, many people find beans easier to digest if you soak them for 24 hours. Remember to drain and refill water every 8–12 hours if soaking for long periods. The hotter the room temperature, the more frequently you should drain and refill the water.

1. Rub beef with salt and pepper and set aside.
2. Add bacon to a large soup pot on medium heat. Once the bacon is floppy, add approximately 1 tablespoon of olive oil and chorizo. Brown the surface of the bacon and sausage.
3. Add onion and sauté until clear. Add garlic. Cook for 1 minute.
4. Discard the soaking water and transfer beans to a pot. Stir.
5. Add stock, pork, beef, and bay leaves. Bring mixture to a slow simmer. Skim off fat that rises to the surface, then lower the heat.
6. Cook for approximately 40 minutes, or until the beans are almost tender. You may need to periodically skim the foam off.
7. Add salt and pepper.
8. Add potatoes and turnip. Cook on medium-low for 15 minutes.
9. Add greens. Cook for an additional 20 minutes, stirring occasionally.
10. Remove from the heat.
11. Remove bay leaves, beef, and ham. When cool, shred the meat and transfer back into the pot. Discard bay leaves.
12. Thicken the soup by removing a few potatoes and beans along with a bit of liquid and smashing together. Add it back to the soup.
13. The last touch is to add a drizzle (*"un chorrito"*) of extra virgin olive oil and stir.

MIRA

Former ReWA Finance Director • Ukraine

Mira Manusova and her daughter emigrated from Ukraine to the US in 1992. She worked as the chief of the communications department in the Ukrainian government but had to leave due to the Chernobyl disaster and other circumstances. In 1995, she started working at ReWA as a finance coordinator and worked her way up to the position of finance director in 2002. Mira saw America as "a land of big dreams," and she wanted her kids to experience it. She retired in 2018 and feels like she achieved her dreams: "Those dreams came true for me. Look, my granddaughter is a lawyer here."

Yield: 4–6 servings

Golubtsi

Provided by Mira Manusova, former ReWA Finance Director

Golubtsi, a stuffed cabbage dish from Ukraine, makes a wonderful and hearty meal, particularly in the midst of a cold winter. Enjoying golubtsi with her family brings back happy childhood memories for Mira.

INGREDIENTS

1 cup white rice

3½ tablespoons olive oil, divided

1½ tablespoons salt, divided

¼ cup white vinegar

1 large green cabbage

1 pound ground turkey or beef

1 large onion, chopped

1 clove garlic, minced

2 celery stalks with leaves, chopped

3 medium carrots, peeled, grated, and divided

1 tablespoon butter

1 large egg

1 tablespoon dried parsley

3½ cups tomato sauce or tomato puree

½ teaspoon pepper

1 tablespoon sour cream, plus more for garnish

1. Rinse white rice until the water runs clear. Bring 3 cups of water, 1 tablespoon olive oil, and ½ teaspoon salt to a boil in a medium saucepan. Add rice. Cover and reduce to a simmer. Cook for 15–20 minutes or until all the water is absorbed.
2. For the cabbage, bring 2 quarts of water to a boil in a large stock pot. Add 1½ teaspoons salt and the vinegar.
3. Use a sharp knife to cut the core out of the cabbage. Put cabbage in water, cored-side down. Cook 2–3 minutes, or until outer leaves are bright green and tender. Lift cabbage from water and place on cutting board. Carefully cut off softened outer leaves from the base of the cabbage. Reserve the leaves.
4. Add the remaining cabbage back into the boiling water, and repeat the process of cooking for 2–3 minutes. Remove from the water to harvest leaves. Repeat this process until all the leaves are cooked to a bright-green color and turn tender.

5. Reserve the cabbage cooking water. Trim down the thick rib from each leaf without cutting through it. This makes the leaf more pliable and the thickness more consistent, like a tortilla. Reserve 4 of the largest leaves to line the bottom of the pan.

6. Set aside the cabbage.

7. For stuffing: Mix the raw ground meat and rice together in a large bowl. Sauté onion, garlic, celery, and ⅔ of grated carrots in 1½ tablespoons oil and 1 tablespoon butter over medium-high heat until soft.

8. Add carrot and celery mixture to the rice and meat. Add 1 egg, 1½ teaspoon salt, and parsley. Mix well.

9. Stuff the cooked leaves: Fill each cabbage leaf with about ¼ cup of the meat mixture. Tuck in the sides and seal like a burrito. These are your stuffed cabbage treasures, your golubtsi.

10. Line 5-quart Dutch oven with the 4 largest cabbage leaves. Place each golubtsi inside the Dutch oven, carefully stacking them.

11. For the *podliva* ("sauce" in Urkainian): Heat 1 tablespoon olive oil to medium. Sauté the remaining carrots. Stir-fry until soft. Add tomato sauce, pepper, and 1 tablespoon of sour cream. Sauté for another minute. Add 2 cups of the reserved cabbage water. Stir well to combine.

12. Pour sauce over the golubtsi, and add enough reserved cabbage water to just cover the cabbage. Discard remaining reserved cabbage water.

13. Bring to a light boil, and then cover and simmer for about 1 hour, or until the cabbage leaves are fully cooked.

14. Serve with more sour cream as garnish.

Yield: 4–6 servings

Jinghpaw Shan Hkak

Provided by Zau Bawk, ReWA Employment Case Manager

Jinghpaw shan hkak or Kachin Beef is a signature dish of the Kachin people, one of the many indigenous groups living in Burma. Zau himself is Kachin. At ReWA, Zau is an employment case manager, but back home in Burma, he owned an IT repair shop and was a skilled computer programmer.

Kachin Beef is Zau's favorite. When he cooks it at home for his wife and young children, he serves it with rice. Zau says there have been times in his life when he has considered a professional career as a chef, but so far, he's been content as an amateur.

Traditionally, this dish is made with a lean boneless shoulder cut of beef that is minced. This is a lot of work, but Zau says it's worth it. Garcinia cambogia, also called *Sani si Jahkraw*, is a sour fruit found in Southeast Asia. It can be found in Asian markets, or lime can be substituted.

INGREDIENTS

5 cloves garlic
1½ inches ginger, peeled
5 Thai chilis (for milder flavor, halve and remove seeds)
2 cups cilantro leaves
1 teaspoon ground turmeric
½ teaspoon black pepper
¼ teaspoon ground Szechuan peppercorn
1 teaspoon ground coriander
1½ teaspoons salt
½-ounce dried garcinia cambogia (the juice of 1 lime can be used as a substitute)
2 pounds lean boneless beef shoulder, minced with a sharp knife

2 generous handfuls of *rau ram* leaves
8 leaves *ngo gai* (Vietnamese cilantro), white ends removed and finely chopped
3 teaspoons vegetable oil

Garnish

3 additional leaves of ngo gai, chopped
1 cup cilantro, chopped

1. Using a mortar and pestle, grind together garlic, ginger, chilis, and cilantro.
2. Add turmeric, black pepper, Szechuan peppercorn powder, coriander, salt, and garcinia cambogia, if using. Grind into a paste. If you are not using garcinia cambogia, add lime juice now and mix well.
3. Heat a nonstick pan over high heat and add beef. Sear.
4. Add spice paste mixture to the pan. Mix well.
5. Add rau ram, ngo gai, and oil to pan. Cook for 5 more minutes.
6. Lower heat to medium-high. Add 2 cups of cold water and bring it to a boil.
7. Cover the pan and cook for 10 minutes, stirring twice to separate the meat.
8. After 10 minutes, remove the lid. Cook until the water has evaporated.
9. Garnish with ngo gai and cilantro. Serve hot.

JINAN

ReWA Student • Iraq

Jinan came from Baghdad, Iraq, to the US five years ago with her husband and four children. Their fifth child was born after they moved.

In Iraq, Jinan's husband worked as a driver while she stayed home, caring for the house and children.

When Jinan left Baghdad, she left behind four sisters and four brothers. A fifth brother died in 2007. She's able to speak with her sisters by phone once a month.

When the family first arrived, they stayed with a friend of Jinan's husband and then got an apartment in Burien. Neither Jinan nor her husband spoke English. It took him about five months before he found a job. He's now a driver for a car rental agency at the airport.

Although Jinan left school at fifteen, her children are ambitious—her fourteen-year-old daughter wants to be a doctor and her twelve-year-old son wants to be an engineer. Jinan's husband and children are happy in the US, and would like to stay. The children prefer to speak English now, and her seven-year-old son can't even read or write Arabic, which makes Jinan sad. If it were safe, Jinan would prefer to return home—but for now, she and her husband are saving money to move into a house, and Jinan finds support at ReWA.

Yield: 15 servings

Dolmas

Provided by Jinan, ReWA Student

Jinan's mother taught her how to make dolmas when she was a teenager living in Iraq. Now, Jinan makes this recipe about twice a month, generally on Fridays. She always makes it for family and community celebrations, including Eid parties, and enjoys sharing it with her ReWA friends and teachers during class potlucks as well.

This recipe differs from the dolmas known to most Americans as stuffed grape leaves. Swiss chard leaves are often substituted for grape leaves in the winter months.

INGREDIENTS

Filling

1 cup basmati rice
2 pounds beef or lamb, finely
   minced or ground
1 cup tomato sauce, divided
2 tablespoons tomato paste
10 shallots, outer layers removed
   and reserved, finely diced
2 cloves garlic, minced
2 large tomatoes, chopped
1 cup Swiss chard, stems removed
   and reserved, chopped
2 teaspoons salt
1 teaspoon black pepper
1 teaspoon cumin
1 teaspoon paprika

½ teaspoon ground coriander
½ teaspoon ground cloves
½ teaspoon ground nutmeg
½ teaspoon cinnamon
1 pinch cardamom
½ cup lemon juice
⅔ cup mild vegetable oil
1½ cup water

For Stuffing

3 green bell peppers
3 small zucchinis
5 small eggplant
Reserved outer layers of 10 shallots
1 (16-ounce) jar of grape
   leaves in brine, rinsed

1. Wash the rice three times, discarding water after each wash. Drain in a colander.
2. To make the filling, in a large bowl, mix together the uncooked rice, minced meat, ½ cup tomato sauce, tomato paste, diced shallots, garlic, tomato, chard greens, salt, pepper, spices, and lemon juice.
3. Remove the stem from bell peppers to create a hole on the top. With a small, sharp knife, remove seeds and whitish ribs inside the peppers. Try to keep the bell pepper intact. Repeat the same process with zucchinis and eggplant—hollowing out each vegetable to allow for filling.
4. Stuff the rice, reserved shallot layers, and the meat mixture inside the vegetables.
5. To stuff grape leaves, place 1 tablespoon of the filling in the center. Fold the sides to the center and fold the leaf over and roll lightly.
6. Place reserved chard stems on the bottom of a pot just wide enough so that all stuffed vegetables fit snugly inside. Place stuffed grape leaves on top of vegetables, seam side down. Add water, remainder of tomato sauce, and oil. Cover the pot with a heat-proof plate.
7. Cook on the stove over low heat for 20 minutes, adding more water if necessary to prevent scorching. Increase the heat to medium for 30 more minutes. Check the water level periodically to make sure the bottom of the vegetables do not burn. Dolmas are ready to eat when the rice stuffing is cooked through.

A Taste of Home

DESSERTS AND DRINKS

Yield: 10–12 servings

Konafa

Provided by Reyad, ReWA Student

In Homs, Syria, where Reyad is from, he worked in the family bakery that had been passed down from his grandfather. They baked and sold many kinds of Mediterranean pastries, including *konafa*, a cheese-filled dessert made with shredded filo.

Reyad still enjoys baking. Not long after he arrived here as a refugee, he remembers inviting a Syrian friend to eat at his house and serving him konafa. His friend said eating the delicious dessert brought back good memories of their home country, and even made Reyad's friend feel like he was back in Syria again.

INGREDIENTS

Syrup
1½ cups water
2 cups sugar
Juice of half a lemon
½ teaspoon vanilla or 2 teaspoons
  orange blossom water

Cheese Layer
1 cup whole-milk ricotta
2 tablespoons sugar

2–3 tablespoons whole milk
2 tablespoons mascarpone cream
1 (16-ounce) package *kataifi*
  (shredded filo dough) or shred
  regular filo dough with a knife
1 cup ghee or clarified butter,
  plus 1½ tablespoons
1 teaspoon kunafa red coloring
  powder (optional)
½ cup pistachio nuts, chopped, for garnish

1. The day before making the dessert, place frozen kataifi in the fridge for 8 hours to thaw. Then leave on the counter for 2 hours at room temperature before using.
2. Preheat oven to 350°F.
3. To make the syrup, combine water and sugar in a saucepan. Cook over medium heat, stirring occasionally, until the sugar is dissolved and a syrup forms.
4. Cook for 5 minutes longer, stirring. During this time, the syrup will become thicker.

5. Add lemon juice and vanilla or orange blossom water. Cook for another 2 minutes. Turn off heat, set aside, and allow to cool to room temperature. Syrup should be completely cooled before using on the hot pastry.

6. To use kataifi, the long pastry threads need to be slightly shredded. Put kataifi in a bowl and pull apart with hands. Then cut threads by hand with kitchen scissors or in a food processor.

7. If using a food processor, put kataifi inside, close lid, and pulse (use the sharp edge of the blade). While pulsing, gradually add 1 cup ghee or clarified butter in 1 tablespoon increments. If cutting with kitchen scissors, make pieces about 1 inch long. Add to a large bowl. Drizzle the ghee or clarified butter into the bowl, then use your fingers to evenly distribute throughout.

8. Transfer the kataifi mixture into a frying pan and brown on medium heat for about 4 minutes to slightly toast the mixture.

9. For the sweet cheese, combine ricotta, sugar, and mascarpone cream. Add just enough milk to make the liquid mixture pourable, and then set aside.

10. Generously grease a large round 8- to 9-inch aluminum pan (or a large quiche pan) with 1½ tablespoons ghee or clarified butter. If using coloring powder, pour the powder on the ghee, spread the ghee and powder evenly on the bottom of the baking pan.

11. Put ⅔ of the kataifi mixture into the baking pan. Press the mixture across the bottom of the pan with your hands or the flat base of a cup. Add the sweet cheese in an even layer on top of the kataifi. Add the remainder of the kataifi mixture evenly over the cheese layer and press this on the top of the cheese layer.

12. Place the pan on the middle rack of the oven. Bake for 20 minutes until the edges are golden brown. At the end, broil for 1–2 minutes to get a nice light brown color.

13. Remove from the oven. While the pastry is hot, pour half of the cooled syrup in circles over the pastry. Let it rest for about 10 minutes, or until the syrup is absorbed.

14. Put a serving plate upside down on top of the baking pan and flip the pan and plate over gently so the konafa falls onto the serving plate. Cut into rectangles or diamonds and sprinkle with chopped pistachios. If desired, add more syrup to further sweeten the dessert.

SAMI

Current Employee, Former ReWA Student • Fijian

Sami's great-grandparents immigrated to Fiji from India, where the family were considered Indo-Fijian people. In Fiji, the economy is fueled by tourism, so after completing high school Sami worked at hotels and airports as a tourism coordinator. Her husband received a degree in engineering and worked in hotel construction.

Sami's sister left Fiji first due to the political situation—winning the green card lottery. She sponsored Sami, who was able to get asylum for herself and her two daughters in 2009. In 2010, Sami was able to do the same for her husband—allowing the family to be reunited. In 2018, Sami and her husband became US citizens.

Since moving to Seattle, ReWA has been a huge part of her life. They even threw her a party to celebrate when she received her citizenship. Sami started at ReWA as a student and after a year she was offered a staff position as a receptionist. She now works as an office coordinator and billing specialist.

"I feel really proud of my achievements."

Yield: Approximately 60

Gulab Jamun

Provided by Sami, ReWA SeaTac Office Coordinator

Gulab jamun is an Indian delicacy consisting of cardamom-scented fried dough dipped in sugar syrup, and it holds a special place in Fiji-born Sami's heart since it is the first thing her mother taught her to make. "It is made during the festival of Diwali," she said, "which holds massive memories of love and contentment. It will forever be an important part of my life." Sami looks forward to the day when she can teach her two young daughters to make gulab jamun and re-create the wonderful experience she had with her own mother.

INGREDIENTS

1 can (14 ounces) sweetened
   condensed milk
1 teaspoon ground cardamom
2 cups and 2 tablespoons ghee, divided

5 tablespoons powdered milk
3½ cups self-rising flour, sifted
3 cups sugar
3 cups water

1. Pour condensed milk into a medium-sized mixing bowl.
2. Add cardamom, 2 tablespoons of ghee, and powdered milk. Whisk until frothy.
3. Add flour to the mixture, ½ cup at a time. Mix with your hands, until a stiff, but pliable dough forms. You may not need to use all of the flour.
4. Form dough into 2-inch-long oblong balls and place on a greased tray; cover and set aside.
5. In the meantime, prepare the sugar syrup. Combine the sugar and water in a saucepan and cook over high heat until the sugar dissolves. Turn down heat and simmer until mixture begins to thicken. Remove from the heat and set aside.
6. Heat 2 cups ghee in a heavy pot for frying over medium-high heat. To check if it is ready, drop a small amount of dough into the hot ghee. It is ready if the tiny bit of dough floats.
7. Fry the dough in small batches until golden brown, turning halfway through.
8. Remove from ghee and drain on paper towels. Allow to cool slightly before placing in sugar syrup. Simmer for 5 minutes.

Yield: 1 sheet cake

Basbousa

Provided by Feras and Basel, ReWA Students

Feras and Basel became friends in ReWA's ESL program after both arriving in the Northwest as refugees from Syria. When he lived in his home country, Feras was a chef in a pastry and nut-roasting shop while working to put himself through a nursing program in college. Basel worked as a blacksmith in Syria, but he has been a passionate home cook for many years.

INGREDIENTS

Cake

2 cups white flour

2 cups coconut flour, fine, plus
    more for decorating

2 cups semolina flour, fine

2 teaspoons baking powder

4 eggs

1 cup sugar

1 cup whole-milk yogurt

1 cup whole milk

1 cup mild vegetable oil

A pinch of salt

2 teaspoons vanilla

¼ (12-ounce) can of orange soda,
    such as Fanta or Crush

2 tablespoons ghee

Syrup

2½ cups sugar

1 cup water

1 teaspoon lemon juice

1. Preheat the oven to 300°F.
2. In a large bowl, sift the white, coconut, and semolina flours and baking powder together three times. Set aside.
3. In separate bowl, add eggs, sugar, yogurt, milk, oil, and a pinch of salt. Beat with an electric mixer for 3 minutes.
4. Add flours to the egg mixture. Add vanilla and orange soda. Beat with the mixer for 2 more minutes.

5. Grease a half sheet pan with ghee. Pour the batter into the pan. Gently shake the pan and lightly tap it on a surface to eliminate any air bubbles in the dough.

6. Place the pan on a rack in the lower half of the oven. Bake for 15 minutes. Rotate the pan for even baking. Bake for 5–10 more minutes. Use a cake tester to determine when it is fully baked. Remove from the oven as soon as the tester comes out dry.

7. While the cake is baking, make a simple syrup. Combine sugar and water in heavy-bottomed pot on the stove. Bring to a boil, stirring constantly. Once the mixture starts to boil, add lemon juice. Reduce the heat to a simmer for 2 more minutes. Remove from the heat.

8. After taking the cake out of the oven, slowly pour the sugar syrup over the cake's surface. Using a sifter, dust the top of the cake with coconut flour. Cool for 2 hours before cutting.

MAS

ReWA Supporter • Malaysia

Mas Puteh and her husband made the decision to come to the US in 1999 for a specific health-care therapy. Their second child was born with classic autism, and the doctors they saw in Malaysia knew very little about the condition. They saw their son languishing but knew that overseas in America doctors were making breakthroughs in autism therapy. When Mas's husband was offered a Malaysian government position in Orlando, Florida, they decided to pack up their family of six and take a chance on the promise of a better life for their son. Their whole family is happy that he was able to attend a special school for students with autism for many years and graduate from the program after reaching adulthood.

Mas first began cooking Malaysian foods to ease the homesickness that she and her husband felt. She found it was a way to develop a community of Malaysian expats wherever she and her family moved. Soon, her friends realized what an excellent cook she was and began asking her to make dishes for them. She never made an actual business out of her cooking skills because her adult son with autism is still dependent on her for care, but she still receives very regular requests from friends to cook and bake for them.

Kuih Seri Muka

Provided by Mas Puteh, ReWA Supporter

Kuih seri muka, which translates to "radiant face dessert," is well known throughout Malaysia, especially at wedding receptions and Eid celebrations, where guests look forward to seeing its fresh, bright-green pandan "face." Mas never tried to make it when she lived in Malaysia. In fact, she says she rarely cooked elaborate meals when she lived there. It was only after she and her husband moved to the US—and she was homesick for her mother's cooking—that she began trying to teach herself to make traditional Malaysian dishes. She particularly missed this very popular dessert and set a goal for herself to learn to make it well. Her recipe is so beloved by her expat friends that they place regular orders.

This is a finicky dessert to master. Follow the steps carefully.

INGREDIENTS

Top Layer (Custard)
5 tablespoons pandan
   extract (recipe follows)
1¼ cups all-purpose white flour
⅞ cup white sugar
2½ cups coconut milk
2 extra-large eggs, plus 1 egg yolk
¾ teaspoon salt

Corn flour, divided into 4
   tablespoons and 1 teaspoon

Bottom Layer (Rice)
3¾ cups of glutinous rice
½ cup coconut milk
1⅛ teaspoons salt

Custard

1. Add 5 tablespoons pandan extract to a liquid measuring cup. Slowly add cold water until the liquid level reaches 1 cup.
2. Add pandan solution, an additional ¾ cup water, and the remaining custard ingredients into a bowl. Mix well with an electric mixer.

3. Place a colander over a heavy-bottomed pot and strain the mixture through it. Gently press any remaining mixture through bottom of colander into the pot.
4. Heat the pot on medium-low. Stir constantly. Once steam starts to rise from the mixture, set a timer for 1 minute. Continue stirring for the remaining minute, and then remove from the heat. Continuing stirring for 3 more minutes. Set aside.

Rice

1. Wash the rice three times, draining off the water completely after each wash. Refill the bowl with water and allow the rice to soak for 30 minutes. Drain the water.
2. Add coconut milk, water, and salt to the bowl with rice. Mix well by hand. Transfer to a large heat-proof dish, such as Pyrex.
3. Steam rice mixture for 25 minutes, either by using a steamer pot set or by placing a steamer insert into a heavy pot. Replenish water if necessary.
4. For the next step, Mas uses 3 smaller heat-proof Pyrex glass dishes, each sized 6 x 8 inches. Grease the dishes lightly with vegetable oil.
5. Divide the rice mixture equally between the 3 dishes.
6. Press firmly down on the rice with the back of a spatula or turner to create a dense compact bottom layer for the dessert.
7. Using a butter knife, very lightly draw a grid of lines across the surface of each rice layer. Cut down into the rice less than ⅛-inch deep. This grid or cross-hatching on the surface of the rice will help the green custard layer stick to the white rice layer after the second round of steaming.

Assembly

Combine the bottom and top layers. *Repeat the following steps for each of the 3 Pyrex dishes:*

1. Pour ⅓ of the green custard mixture over the rice in one dish. Add more water to the steamer pot. Place one small Pyrex dish in the top steamer insert of the steamer set. (The other two Pyrex baking dishes with the rice layer can sit out at room temperature, covered, while you prepare and steam the first dish. Store the remaining green custard in the refrigerator while the first dish is steaming.)
2. Do not cover the steamer insert with the pot lid. Instead, cover the top of the insert with a dishtowel. This should help the custard develop a smooth and flat surface. If you were to use the pot lid, condensation would form on the underside of the lid, which would then drop down onto the custard, making the surface uneven.

3. Steam on medium-high for 32 minutes.

4. After 32 minutes, remove the kitchen towel. Being careful not to burn your hands, move the Pyrex dish within the steamer insert until it is resting against one side of the steamer insert. (This prevents the dish from moving on its own when you follow the next step.) Tilt the complete steamer set slightly toward you to drain any water off the top of the custard. The custard layer should already be set, so it should not move as you tilt the pot.

5. Replace pot on stove burner. Continue steaming for 8 more minutes uncovered. The top of the green layer should dry out.

6. Carefully remove the Pyrex from the steamer. You can either cool the kuih seri muka naturally for 3–4 hours (cover it lightly with foil or a second dishtowel), or you can speed up the cooling process by placing it in a larger pan of cold water for 1½–2 hours; leave it covered with foil. Once cool, cut kuih seri muka with a sharp knife into rectangles sized 2 by 1½ inches.

Store in a tightly sealed container in a cool space protected from direct sunlight and consume within three days. Ideally, kuih seri muka should not be refrigerated.

Yield: 6–7 tablespoons

Pandan Extract

Provided by Mas Puteh, ReWA Supporter

Mas is a highly respected home cook in the Malaysian expat community of the greater Seattle area. Her food is so beloved, and she enjoys cooking so much, that her friends regularly "order" dishes and desserts from her. In her opinion, it is worth taking the extra time to make your pandan extract from scratch. She has developed this simple process for those living in regions of the world where it is difficult—or impossible—to attain fresh pandan leaves. The resulting liquid is a brilliant green extract with a heady scent and delightful floral flavor.

INGREDIENTS

1 (7-ounce) bag of frozen pandan leaves

1. Wash the leaves, cut off any white parts at the base of the leaves, and cut each leaf into inch-long pieces.
2. Put the pandan leaves in a blender jar and add enough cold water to just cover the leaves. Blend until very fine.
3. Strain the mixture through cheesecloth or a tea-leaf strainer, gently squeezing the leaves within the cloth to extract all of the liquid.
4. Transfer the liquid to a glass jar. Cover the jar and allow to sit in the refrigerator for 3 hours.
5. The water will separate from the green extract. After 3 hours, gently pour out most (about 80 percent) of the water, leaving the thick pandan extract.
6. If you do not plan to use your pandan extract within a day, freeze small portions for future use.

YENNHI

ReWA Naturalization Case Manager and Domestic Violence Survivor's Advocate • Vietnam

A native of Saigon, Yennhi (*pronounced Ing-yee*) Le was only twenty-six years old when, fearing persecution in their own country, she and her husband fled to Malaysia, where they spent two years in a refugee camp on one of the islands before being transferred to another refugee camp on the mainland, where they remained for another five years.

Yennhi worked hard throughout her years in the refugee camps. On the island, she worked for a women's program, advising other women on health issues. On the mainland, she worked in an elementary school for refugee children, teaching subjects like reading, writing, and math.

Through the UN refugee resettlement program, Yennhi and her husband eventually moved to Seattle, arriving with their ten-month-old son on October 31, 1998. The resettlement volunteers brought them to their first home in the US and showed them how to use the lights and appliances. After presenting them with a refrigerator stocked with food, the volunteers left them.

That evening after dusk, Yennhi and her husband heard a knock on the door. Her husband opened the door cautiously and peered out, with Yennhi looking on from behind. He quickly slammed the door shut, jumping back.

Yennhi and her husband looked at each other in shock and fright. They had never before seen such a strangely dressed group of people. "Is this what Americans really look like?" Yennhi asked in disbelief.

It was only later that they could laugh off their initial fear, when they learned that the group of older children standing at their new door were costumed trick-or-treaters!

After she learned enough English, Yennhi enrolled in community college. She now holds an associate's degree in accounting, another in business information, and a medical clerk's certificate.

Yennhi still helps people as she did in the refugee camps. A staff member of ReWA since 2006, she loves working with people with backgrounds similar to her own, and finds it very rewarding when her clients' applications for green cards and US citizenship are successful. Today, she and her husband are the parents of two University of Washington students. One of their sons is studying urban planning, and the other son is studying psychology. One of Yennhi's proudest moments was when one of her sons came home from middle school with the assignment to write a paper on the life of his hero. He chose to write about his mother.

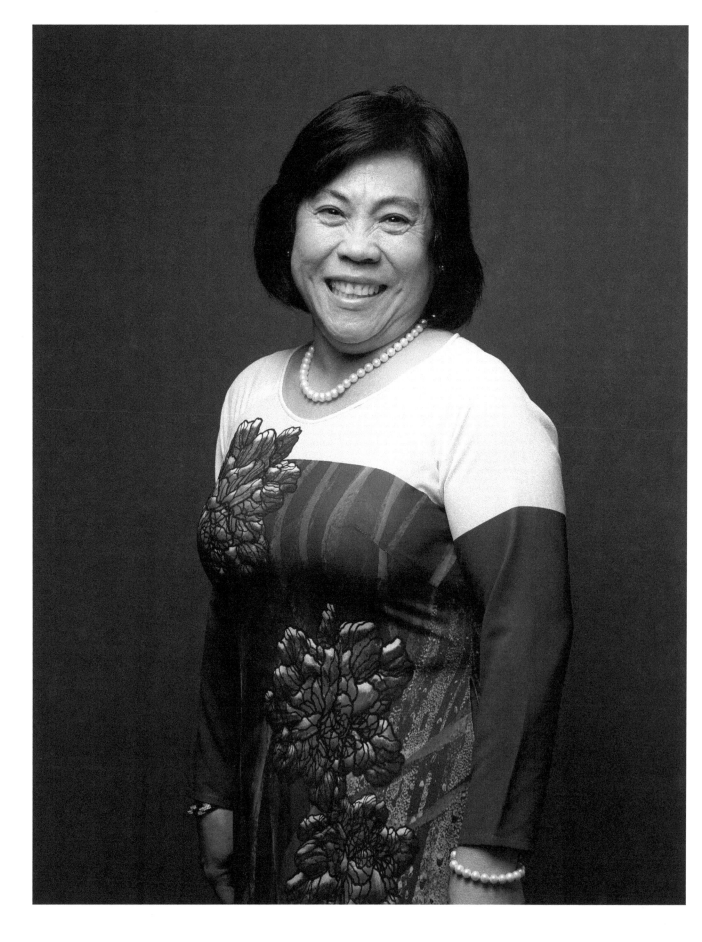

Yield: 2 dozen, depending on size of the mold

Banh Phuc Linh

Provided by Yennhi Le (pronounced Ing-yee Lee), ReWA Naturalization Case Manager and Domestic Violence Survivor's Advocate

Banh phuc linh are melt-in-your-mouth pastel cookies that are a popular treat to serve at Tết, the Vietnamese New Year. When Yennhi was twelve years old, she, her sister, and two friends decided this cookie was their ticket to financial independence. They baked several beautiful batches, arranged the cookies on platters, and brought them to the big market near their home in Saigon. While waiting for their customers to arrive, they set down the platters and started playing. Suddenly, a strong wind picked up, blowing over every plate. The girls' business went bankrupt before they could sell their first cookie!

INGREDIENTS

1⅓ cups tapioca flour, plus
    more for dusting molds
3 pandan leaves, blotted dry
1¼ cup powdered sugar, plus
    more for dusting
⅔ cup coconut milk

1 tablespoon beet powder, for
    coloring (optional)
1 tablespoon pandan extract,
    for coloring (optional)
1- to 2-inch cookie mold*

1. Preheat oven to 200°F.
2. Spread 1⅓ cups tapioca flour in a 9- by 13-inch glass baking dish. Set aside.
3. Cut pandan leaves into 3-inch pieces. Mix leaves with the tapioca flour. Bake for 1 hour, or until the leaves are crisp.
4. If you are choosing to color your cookies, do so now. To make pink cookies, whisk 1 tablespoon beet powder into the coconut milk. To make light green cookies, stir 1 tablespoon liquid pandan extract into the coconut milk. Use enough to achieve the desired color intensity.
5. Remove pandan leaves from the flour and discard. Add flour and powdered sugar to food processor and pulse to mix well. Add coconut milk 2 teaspoons at a time to this flour mixture, pulsing in between additions. Note: the dough will not come together

as in Western-style cookie recipes. It will appear more like a dense powder. After each addition, pinch the dough and see whether it holds its shape. Once it does, it's ready for shaping.

6. Add a slight dusting of tapioca flour to cookie molds and dump out the excess flour. Slightly overfill each mold with the dough, then press mold cover down to pack each cookie tightly. Turn the mold upside down to physically press the two halves of the mold together firmly between your fingers. Turn mold right-side up and remove mold cover. Use a toothpick to clean the edges of the mold so your cookie edge is crisp.

7. Release cookies from mold by turning bottom piece upside down on your prep surface, then tap lightly on the bottom of the mold until the cookie drops out. If your cookies are broken, or do not have crisp, clean edges, you have not added enough coconut milk to your dough. Return all cookie dough to the food processor, add 2 teaspoons more coconut milk, and repeat the previous steps.

8. Arrange cookies on a lovely platter, dust with powdered sugar, and enjoy!

*Note: You will need a silicone or plastic cookie mold to form the dough. Yennhi likes to use a plastic sushi rice mold as it forms a denser cookie that holds together well. The Imonata 1506 Sushi Mold Rice Ball Maker with Three Shapes is available online.

Yield: 90 1-inch cookies

Nan-e Berenji

Provided by Mahnaz Eshetu, ReWA Executive Director

These bite-size cookies are a Persian classic that are subtly sweet, simple to make, and gluten-free.

INGREDIENTS

Syrup
¾ cup sugar
¼ cup water
¼ teaspoon rose water

Cookies
¾ teaspoon sugar

1 egg yolk
1 cup finely ground white rice flour
⅓ cup clarified butter
2½ tablespoons mild vegetable oil
½ teaspoon ground cardamom
Poppy seeds, for decoration

1. Preheat oven to 350°F.
2. Combine sugar and ¼ cup water in small, heavy-bottomed pan over high heat.
3. Stir for about 3 minutes until the sugar dissolves.
4. Remove from the heat and add rose water. Cool to room temperature before using. Set aside.
5. In a separate bowl, combine the sugar and egg yolk. Beat until creamy. Set aside.
6. In another bowl, combine rice flour, clarified butter, oil, and cardamom.
7. Add to sugar-yolk mixture and combine.
8. Add ¼ cup of syrup and mix until combined.
9. Cover and refrigerate for at least 30 minutes.
10. Roll dough into balls about ¾ inch in diameter and place on baking sheets lined with parchment paper.
11. Flatten each ball and sprinkle with poppy seeds.
12. Bake for 5 minutes. Rotate sheet front to back in oven. Bake for 5 more minutes.
13. Cool to room temperature on baking sheet before removing.

Yield: 35 cookies

Nan-e Nokhodchi

Provided by Mahnaz Eshetu, ReWA Executive Director

These tender cookies are traditionally baked for the Persian New Year, *Nowruz*. These are similar to a shortbread—crumbly and sandy, with a melt-in-your-mouth texture. The flavors of cardamom, rose water, and pistachios lend a delicious complexity. They are traditionally cut into a miniature clover shape, but any small cookie cutter will work. The gluten-free roasted chickpea flour can be found at Middle Eastern markets.

INGREDIENTS

1 cup clarified butter
1½ cups confectioner's sugar
3 teaspoons ground cardamom
¼ teaspoon fine sea salt

1 tablespoon rose water
3½ cups roasted chickpea flour, sifted
   three times, plus more for dusting
¼ cup raw pistachio slivers, for garnish

1. Preheat oven to 300°F.
2. Combine butter, sugar, cardamom, salt, and rose water in the bowl of a stand mixer or use a hand-held beater. Beat on low, then gradually increase the speed to as high as it will go without splashing mixture over the edge of the bowl. Cream together for 5 minutes, and then stop beating and scrape dough down the sides.
3. Add chickpea flour and beat on low for 1 minute. If the dough is sticky, gradually add a little more chickpea flour. Do not overmix.
4. Line a baking sheet with parchment paper and dust with chickpea flour. Remove dough to the lined baking sheet and knead gently into a ball.
5. Using a rolling pin, flatten dough into a square, ¾-inch thick. Cover with plastic wrap and refrigerate for at least 1 hour.
6. When ready to bake, line two additional baking sheets with parchment.
7. Remove dough from refrigerator and remove plastic wrap. Using a cutter in your desired shape, cut out as many cookies as possible from the chilled dough. Spacing at least ½-inch apart, transfer cookies to the parchment-lined baking sheets using a thin spatula. Garnish with pistachio slivers.

8. Gather together scraps and re-roll, cutting out cookies until the dough is all used up.
9. Bake for 25–30 minutes or until the cookies turn a light golden brown. Allow the cookies to cool on the baking sheet set on a wire rack.
10. Once cookies are completely cool, gently transfer to a serving platter.

IAD AND SAFA

ReWA Job Training Students and Owners of Alati Souq Catering, Syrian Food • Syria

Iad Senan Alati and Safa Jneidi's journey from Syria isn't just a journey story, it's a love story. The couple fled the war raging in their home country in 2012, arriving as refugees in the US in 2017, the day before the Trump administration first closed our country's borders to all Syrian refugees. It wasn't a good omen for a love story.

But Iad (pronounced *Ee-yad*) remembers clearly the day he first saw Safa. He was working in his family's textile and fabric store, the once famous 400-year-old La Medina Souq, in Aleppo, Syria. He demonstrates with his hands how his heart leapt out of his breast and shot across the space toward Safa, when he saw her browsing in the aisles between the textiles.

In that moment, Safa herself was lost in the Alati family's products, intent on the clothing and fabrics. Educated in fashion and art, Safa immediately appreciated the rich material and gorgeous patterns of the Alati family's wares.

Iad describes making his way quickly through his store on the pretense of assisting Safa with her shopping, while really strategizing about the best way to chat her up. By the time she left, he had figured out how to contact her and to introduce himself to her parents. Three weeks later, the couple was engaged, and ten months later they were married.

The deep love they feel for each other is evident. And now, it's a love forged in triumph over repeated adversity.

Less than two years after their wedding, they were forced to flee Aleppo with their infant daughter when the bombing in that city became relentless. Two hours after showing their passports at the border with Turkey and being allowed entry, they heard and felt the blast that signaled the destruction of the border crossing itself. Today, the location of Iad's family business exists only as a pile of rubble in the middle of a war zone.

The love story continues here in the Pacific Northwest, though. Iad and Safa now have a second beautiful daughter, and they have resurrected the Alati family business as Alati Souq Catering and Alati Souq Textiles. Iad is the head chef in their Syrian food catering business, and Safa imports and sells fine fabrics from the Middle East.

Iad's cooking credentials include his time spent learning the trade in Turkey at a well-known kebab restaurant in Manisa, and his time as a student at Project Feast, a non-profit organization located in Kent, Washington, with the mission of transforming the lives of refugees and immigrants by training them for sustainable jobs in the food industry. Iad takes inspiration from the ancient Turkish entrepreneur who visited Aleppo hundreds of years ago, learned the fine art of baking Syrian baklava, and brought the pastry back with him to Turkey. As Iad describes, the successful businessman's goal was "to spread the culture of food among diverse people." Today, Iad claims this as his own calling.

Both Iad and Safa are ESL and Job Training students at ReWA and are very happy with the life they are now able to provide for their children.

Yield: 60 pieces

Baklava

Provided by Iad Senan Alati, Head Chef at Alati Souq Catering and ReWA Student

According to Iad *(pronounced Ee-yad),* about 200 years ago, a Turkish visitor took his first bite of Syrian baklava and was immediately enchanted by the dessert. He convinced his local hosts to teach him how to bake the delicious pastry and then brought the recipe back to his hometown in Turkey. That young entrepreneur grew his Turkish baklava bakery into a well-known and beloved business.

Iad takes inspiration from that successful businessman's story. Today, baklava is the prized delicacy on the menu at Alati Souq Catering, Iad's own business. While Iad often makes his filo from scratch, he suggests you save time and purchase premade filo. There is a fine art to making homemade filo, and it is time-consuming. Iad and his wife, Safa, are former refugees from Syria and live and work on Vashon Island, Washington.

INGREDIENTS

1 pound filo dough, 12 by 17 inches, thawed in refrigerator overnight and left at room temperature for 2 hours (unopened) prior to assembly

Nut Filling
1 cup granulated sugar
1 pound pistachios, pulsed in the blender
1 pound almonds
1 teaspoon cardamom
1 teaspoon cinnamon

Syrup
1 cup sugar
1 cup honey
1½ teaspoons vanilla
1 cup water
1 tablespoon lemon juice

For Greasing
2 cups ghee

Topping
½ cup or more pistachios, finely chopped

1. Preheat oven to 350°F. Make sure the filling, syrup, and filo are prepared for use before starting to assemble the dish.

2. To make the filling, mix together all the ingredients on a wide, clean cutting surface and finely chop using a heavy knife.
3. To make the syrup, mix together sugar, honey, vanilla, water, and lemon juice in a heavy-bottomed pot.
4. Bring to a boil, then quickly lower heat to bring the mixture to 165°F. Use a candy thermometer to measure the temperature.
5. Hold at 165°F for 15 minutes, stirring occasionally until the mixture thickens.
6. Remove from the heat and allow to cool to room temperature before using, or the baklava will get soggy.
7. To make baklava, brush the rimmed 12- by 18-inch baking pan with ghee.
8. Place one sheet of filo at a time on the pan. Brush the top of each layer with ghee before adding another sheet.
9. After adding 5 layers of filo, add the nut mixture, spreading evenly across all filo layers. Gently press down on the nut mixture so that the height is even throughout pan.
10. Add another 12 layers of filo on top of the nut mixture and brush each layer with ghee.
11. Using a sharp knife, trim any uneven filo edges and tuck under the filo layers. No need to remove trimmings from the pan.
12. Score filo evenly along the long edge into 10 equal pieces. Score filo evenly along the short edge into 6 equal pieces. Cut pan of filo into 60 rectangular pieces.
13. Bake at 350°F for 25 minutes, until golden brown.
14. Just after taking out of the oven, while the pastry is still very hot, pour 1 cup of the room-temperature syrup evenly over the baklava. You will have extra syrup remaining.
15. Sprinkle each piece of baklava with a pinch of chopped pistachios.
16. Let the pastry cool for at least 1 hour before serving.

Yield: 24 pieces

Warbat

Provided by Reyad, ReWA Student

In Syria, there are many different and equally wonderful filo pastry desserts. If you have never worked with filo pastry before, Reyad suggests you learn to work with filo on a small scale. It is easier to handle and grease smaller pieces of filo than the large sheets used in baklava. These 4-inch squares of filo used to make *warbat* may be the perfect (and most delicious) way to start. Before use, thaw frozen filo in the refrigerator overnight and then leave out on the counter 2 hours prior to preparing the dish.

INGREDIENTS

Pastry
20 sheets filo dough, 12 by 17 inches,
    thawed and prepared for use
4 cups whole milk
1¼ cups fine semolina flour
¾ cup grated mozzarella cheese
3½ cups ghee or clarified butter, melted

Syrup
2 cups sugar
¾ cup water
1 teaspoon lemon juice

Garnish
1½ cups pistachios, finely chopped

Pastry

1. Preheat the oven to 300°F.
2. Bring milk to a boil in heavy-bottomed pot on stove. Very gradually, while stirring constantly, add semolina flour to achieve a thick mixture. Stir for about 7–10 minutes.
3. Invert pot onto a clean working surface and allow the dough to fall out and cool to a temperature comfortable for handling.
4. While the dough is cooling, cut each sheet of filo into 12 4-inch squares; discard the trimmings.
5. When cool enough to handle, knead mozzarella cheese into the dough.

6. Brush a large metal baking pan with some ghee.

7. Use 10 squares of filo dough to make each piece of warbat. Working on the surface of the baking pan, lay out as many filo squares as will fit. Brush top sides of each filo square with ghee, layering each new square over the previous square until you have stacks of 10 squares each.

8. Place 1 tablespoon of cheese mixture in the center of each stack. Gently fold filo in half to create a triangle with the cheese mixture inside, gently pressing the warbat into shape. Slide warbat into one corner of pan.

9. Repeat with the remaining squares. Tuck each new warbat pouch next to the previous one, until all the filo has been used.

10. Place the pan in the oven and bake for 30 minutes, or until the edges are crispy.

11. While the warbat is baking, make the sugar syrup by bringing sugar and water to a boil in a heavy-bottomed pot. When it comes to a boil, add lemon juice.

12. Turn the heat down to a simmer. After 2 minutes, remove from the heat and let it cool.

13. Sugar syrup should be no warmer than 100°F when poured over filo pastry.

14. Remove warbat from the oven. Immediately pour cooled syrup over hot filo pastry, drizzling evenly over the pastry.

15. Garnish each warbat with a pinch of chopped pistachios.

Yield: 2 servings

Thai Tea

Provided by Peter Ringold, ReWA Supporter

This classic drink is often served iced as well as warm.

INGREDIENTS

2 tablespoons loose-leaf strong
   black tea (such as Ceylon)
3 cups water
1 whole star anise
2 cardamom seeds

1 tablespoon sugar
2 tablespoons sweetened
   condensed milk, divided
Mint leaves, for garnish

1. In a small pot on the stove, bring tea leaves, water, star anise, cardamom, and sugar to a boil. Immediately remove from the heat and cover.
2. Allow it to steep for 3–5 minutes.
3. Strain tea into two mugs.
4. Stir 1 tablespoon condensed milk into each mug.
5. Garnish with mint.

Shaah

Provided by Rahima, ReWA Volunteer

Somalis enjoy an afternoon tea tradition where they gather to enjoy spiced tea along with savory snacks, such as sambusa, and sweet treats. There are many variations on *shaah*, but all are redolent with warm spices. It is usually served sweet, with or without milk.

INGREDIENTS

14 green cardamom pods

10 whole cloves

2 cinnamon sticks, broken
   into small pieces

1 teaspoon ground ginger

4½ cups water

1 teaspoon black tea leaves

Sugar

Milk

1. Using a mortar and pestle, lightly crush the spices to release their essential oils.
2. Pour water into a medium saucepan. Add all the spices and bring to a boil.
3. Add the tea leaves and lower the heat. Simmer on low for a few minutes, or until the tea turns amber in color.
4. Strain the tea into cups and serve with sugar and/or milk.

Yield: 4 servings

Kawah

Provided by Betina Simmons Blaine, ReWA Bridge Builder Volunteer

Tea is an important part of Afghan hospitality. Chances are that if you visit a home in Afghanistan, you will be offered cup after cup of this spiced green tea. Similar to chai, this tea features spices like cardamom and cinnamon, with the unexpected addition of saffron. *Kawah* is traditionally served from a samovar, a metal urn-like teapot with a spigot at its base.

INGREDIENTS

4 cups water

3 teaspoons dried green tea leaves
(Kashmiri tea is traditional, but feel free to substitute any green tea)

4 green cardamom pods, cracked

1 small stick cinnamon

4 threads saffron

4 blanched almonds, chopped

Honey or sugar

1. Pour the water into a saucepan along with cardamom, cinnamon, and tea leaves and bring to a boil. Simmer for 5 minutes.
2. Remove from the heat and add saffron. Cover and steep for about 3 minutes.
3. Strain tea and add honey or sugar as desired. Add chopped almonds to each cup and serve hot.

SUPRIYA

ReWA Volunteer • India

Supriya has volunteered for ReWA and attended ReWA events since 2000, the same year she moved to the US. She worked on ReWA's first capital campaign at that time to construct a new headquarters building. Before the construction project, ReWA operated out of a tiny yellow structure located in the Seattle Housing Authority Rainier Vista property along Martin Luther King Jr. Way South. The light rail was scheduled to come through the Rainier Valley, and the city had to repossess some of the land where the building sat, meaning the organization had to find a new home. Today, the ReWA family considers the move fortuitous, as it allowed them to grow by leaps and bounds. They would not have been successful were it not for committed project volunteers like Supriya.

Yield: 2 cups

Sambhaaram

Provided by Supriya Unnikrishnan, ReWA Volunteer

Sambhaaram is a cold milky drink, similar to the well-known Indian yogurt drink called *lassi*—but that's where the similarity ends, according to Supriya. The recipe is a specialty of Kerala in southern India, the home of Supriya's ancestral family. Try it on a hot, sunny day!

INGREDIENTS

1 cup cold buttermilk
½ cup water
½-inch fresh ginger

¼ piece jalapeño, with seeds only if you dare! (other green peppers can be used as a substitute)
Salt to taste
5 whole curry leaves (optional)

1. Blend all ingredients together in a blender. Drink as is, or strain through a small colander if you prefer a smooth drink.

Yield: 2 large cups

Spicy Black Ginger Tea

Provided by Supriya Unnikrishnan, ReWA Volunteer

Many westerners are familiar with Indian chai, which tends to use a set of specific spices. However, many Indian households and regions have developed their own special blend of spices and recipes for making spiced tea. Supriya, an immigrant from India, is also a longtime ReWA supporter and former volunteer. In fact, she first started volunteering at ReWA in 2000, the same year she moved to this country. The rest of her family remains in India, though. Refining and sharing recipes like this one—with adopted family and friends in this new country—has helped her find a new sense of belonging. She also says sipping a steaming cup of spicy tea has been the perfect momentary escape on cold, rainy Seattle days!

INGREDIENTS

2 bags of strong black tea (Supriya often uses PG tips) or 2 heaping teaspoons loose leaf black tea

½–¾ inch fresh ginger, grated

⅓ cup milk

3 cups water

Sugar

Pinch of garam masala (optional)

1. Place 3 cups water in a small pot on the stove. Add ginger and bring to a boil over high heat. Add tea bags or leaves. Return to a boil.
2. Add milk and return to a boil until the tea thickens slightly. Remove from the heat.
3. Remove tea bags and pour the tea into cups or pour through a strainer if using loose-leaf tea.
4. Add sugar and a pinch of garam masala to each cup, if you like.

NAWAAL

ReWA Youth Program Participant, College Student and
Cook at Amazon Cafe in Seattle • Somalia

I was born in Somalia and raised by my aunt in a small village. My only job was to take care of my aunt's goats. From the time I turned six years old, every day I would take them out of their pens at sunrise. Sometimes, if hyenas or lions ate the goats I was caring for, or if I lost a goat in the forest, my aunt would make me sleep outside that night with the goats. She had two hundred goats.

Do you know how it feels to sleep with two hundred goats? The goats would step on me all night if I fell asleep, and it really hurt. Pretty soon, when I realized I had lost a goat, I would run away from home and sleep outside by myself that night, so I didn't have to sleep with the goats.

During the time in my life when I was a goat herder, I didn't know anything about education. At least, not the kind of education you get from books.

When I moved to Nairobi, though, I was able to go school for the first time. I was thirteen years old, and I had to start in first grade. Of course, those kids were much younger than I was. I had never been to school before, and had never read—or even seen—a book. In class, my brain felt dark, like being in a room at night with no light on. I was embarrassed because I was so much older and taller than the other kids.

The day after I arrived in Seattle, I was taken to a school testing center. I was amazed when I was placed into ninth grade, despite the fact that I had only a fourth-grade education at that point. The schoolwork was not as hard as I thought it would be, but I was still struggling to be fluent in English.

I looked for extra help after school. That was how I found ReWA. I got help with my homework here after school, and I also started going to the ReWA job training program to learn job skills and time management. I enjoyed the job-training program so much that I signed up for a second year and became a peer leader.

After graduating from high school, I also joined ReWA's Post-Secondary Success Program, which is why I'm still so connected to ReWA today. ReWA helped me apply to Seattle Central College, where I'm currently in my second year.

I feel closer to fulfilling my dreams of becoming a lawyer. I want to be a lawyer to help low-income people fight for affordable housing, and to defend innocent people. I want to be a lawyer so I can help other people the way that ReWA helped me.

Yield: 1–2 servings

Cambuulo

Provided by Nawaal Khalif, ReWA Post-Secondary Success Student in our Youth Program

Cambuulo is a traditional Somali dish of beans and rice, and the term can refer to beans and rice prepared in many different ways. According to Nawaal, while bread and spicy dishes would traditionally be eaten for breakfast or lunch, rice and beans dishes would typically be eaten for dinner or as an evening snack. Nawaal herself is a college student living on her own and within a budget. She often makes this quick, yet classic version of cambuulo, and considers it her go-to comfort food. While she makes hers with West African brown beans, the dish is sometimes made with adzuki beans, or other varieties. However, Nawaal says she, personally, would never make cambuulo with black beans. In fact, she had never tried black beans before moving to Seattle!

INGREDIENTS

½ cup West African (Nigerian) brown beans (or black-eyed peas, adzuki, or navy beans)

½ cup white or brown long-grain rice

1 tablespoon sugar

1 tablespoon sesame oil

¼ cup milk or heavy cream

1. Fill a medium-sized pot with water and bring to a boil on the stove. Add beans and lower the heat. Simmer, stirring occasionally, for 20 minutes, or until the beans are soft enough to break apart in your fingers.
2. If the water has boiled down too far, add enough so that the beans are covered with water. Add rice to the pot. Continue to simmer and stir until the rice is cooked. Brown rice will take longer than white rice to cook.
3. By this point, the water should be almost fully absorbed or evaporated.
4. Mix well with sugar, sesame oil, and milk or cream.

OUR FOUNDING MOTHERS

"Women aren't perfect, but spaces run by women take on a different sensibility coming out of their 'womaness.'"

—Former ReWA Board Member Wadiyah Nelson-Shimabukuro

Linh Dang Shields

ReWA Founding Mother

Linh Dang was highly educated before she ever left Vietnam. She graduated from the School of Social Work in Saigon and earned two bachelor's degrees, one in French Studies and the second in Vietnamese Studies. She held different positions where her command of multiple languages—including Mandarin, Cantonese, Teochew, Vietnamese, English, and French—made her an asset to her employers.

Linh Dang's eldest sister was an employee of Air America when the communists entered Saigon, and left Saigon on an escape flight. She eventually settled in Seattle. A year after her sister's departure, Linh Dang helped her mother leave for Hong Kong. Gradually, one by one, she helped her other siblings flee the turmoil raging around their family home. They landed scattered around the world, while Linh Dang stayed behind to care for her aging father.

Linh Dang's own journey would take over two years, leaving her country with only twenty dollars to her name, with stops in Ivory Coast and France, where she worked odd jobs to cover her basic needs. The eventual reunion of Linh Dang, her eldest sister, and their parents in Seattle was of immense relief.

When Linh Dang Shields met Emmanuelle Chi Dang in 1983, both women had already endured more upheaval and adventure than anyone should have to face in one lifetime as Vietnamese refugees. It makes sense then, that they were drawn toward one another.

Not content to weep together over the demise of the country and lives they had known, or to simply swap stories of escaping the communist crackdown, the two women had the audacity to want to make the resettlement process easier for other women who arrived in Seattle as refugees. Mrs. Chi shared with Linh Dang her vision of a center where any Southeast Asian woman could seek the advice, support, and English language instruction that would make the transition to this new life a bit easier, and Linh Dang responded excitedly with her own ideas for turning the brilliant idea into a reality.

Think about that for a moment. Linh Dang had immigrated to Seattle *less than one year* before she and her new friend were already drawing up a plan to create a place where other women could gather and find comradery, community, and education. Talk about female empowerment, and in an age when that catch-phrase had yet to be coined.

Theresa Wong

ReWA Founding Mother

When I left Vietnam in 1973 to attend university in Seattle, I could not have known it would be thirty-two years before I would return to my home country. If I had even an inkling of this, I would have packed at least a few childhood photos.

During my junior year at the University of Washington, my status in the eyes of US government officials changed overnight from foreign student to refugee. At that same time, my parents were fleeing Vietnam to escape communist control. Since both my sister and I were students in Seattle, they were eventually able to join us here.

I knew immediately that we were the lucky ones. From thousands of miles away, we watched news coverage of the fall of Saigon and wept over the destruction we saw and the terrible events our friends and neighbors had to endure.

In those days, any little connection to home helped ease the sense of helplessness. It was thrilling then, when less than a decade after I arrived in the States, I ran into one of my

school classmates from Saigon, Thu-Van Nguyen. Soon afterwards, Thu-Van invited me to visit her whole family. Her mother, Mrs. Emmanuelle Chi Dang, had been my middle school English teacher.

At the time, Mrs. Chi was hard at work putting together the group of women who would go on to help her found the South East Asian Women's Alliance. What would you say if your most assertive and principled middle school teacher asked you to help her with a special project? What if, to say no would have felt as if you were shirking some great responsibility? Even though I had a career, a husband, and two young children, I agreed to help.

That work became a real source of pleasure in my life. Looking back on our history, I am proud of what Mrs. Chi, my friends, and I set in place. I am proud of what the many leaders at ReWA have helped to accomplish. And I am always inspired by what refugee women can accomplish.

Of course, I will be happy if readers pick up this cookbook with the intention of exploring new cultures through cuisine. I do hope, though, that the incredible personal stories we share within these pages will touch and inspire readers on an even deeper level, just as I have been inspired time and again by the students, clients, staff, and leaders at ReWA.

Thu-Van Nguyen

ReWa Founding Mother

On one of her last days living in Saigon, Thu-Van recalls sitting in her room listening to the Beatles. Her mother called to her in exasperation from downstairs, "How can you listen to music at a time like this? Don't you know what's going on out there?!" Thu-Van did know that war—which had once raged in the jungles seemingly far away from her big city—was growing closer. As a twenty-one-year-old, cosmopolitan, young woman, it had felt removed from her daily life. Now, though, time spent with the Beatles was a moment of escape from what seemed like impending chaos.

Saigon fell to the North Vietnamese on April 30, 1975.

Thu-Van and her immediate family—eight of them in total—fled Saigon on April 29, 1975. She counts herself as one of the few extremely lucky former residents of that city. Connections can sometimes mean the difference between life and death, and that was certainly the case for her family. One of their close family friends was a commodore in the South Vietnamese navy, with connections in high places. He helped Thu-Van's family escape.

Still, their escape was a tense undertaking. It involved being less than truthful to nearby friends and neighbors, traveling through the city on the backs of electric scooters at dusk—during curfew—being stopped multiple times by soldiers at checkpoints, and telling a fabricated tale designed to allow them to pass. Since those scooters were like Ubers on two wheels, each one had a "driver." So now imagine the group of sixteen—including young children—and their scooter chauffeurs traveling in a bike gang-style pack through those deserted streets. Just a little conspicuous.

Believe it or not, that part of her journey out of the war zone now feels tame compared to what happened next. Thu-Van, her parents, and her five younger siblings soon found themselves skimming over the harbor in the dark on a US Navy patrol boat with about a hundred other people hoping to escape, alongside a massive US battleship. Their Navy escorts were radioing back and forth with the people on the deck above, trying to figure out the best means of getting the civilians from the water level onto the high deck. Thu-Van later learned the distance between the deck of the patrol boat and the deck of the battleship was equivalent to three building stories. At the time, it seemed even greater.

In the end, the sailors on the battleship threw down a wide net. Each would-be escapee had to physically climb that net— like climbing a rope ladder—to reach the battleship above. They made the climb in groups. Thu-Van says the repeated commands of the sailors, from both above and below, still haunt her. "Look up as you climb! Don't look down!" Thu-Van's youngest sibling was nine at the time. There were even younger children in some of the other families who had to make that climb. She remembers the sound of her mother being sick, throwing up as she climbed.

That same mother is the woman who would go on—only ten short years later—to lead a group of former refugee women in an admirable call to action. The organization that became ReWA was Thu-Van's mother's idea. She was determined to create a place where other women like herself and her daughters could seek support and services. She enlisted the help of Thu-Van and other refugee women in the ambitious project and it was highly successful in the end.

In 1987, Thu-Van met her future husband when they were colleagues at Pacific Medical Center here in Seattle. The couple have four grown boys and a large, extended family.

TOGETHER WE ARE ONE

A refugee is someone who has been forced to flee their country because of persecution, war, or violence. A refugee has a well-founded fear of persecution for reasons of race, religion, nationality, political opinion, or membership in a particular social group. Refugees leave behind jobs, houses, and personal possessions and endure great hardship in their fight for safety and survival. Over three quarters of the world's refugees are women and children.

In June 2018, the UN estimated that there were 24.5 million refugees worldwide. Refugees exist throughout the world in areas of conflict.

The U.S. accepts a limited number of refugees each year. In 2018 the U.S. will allow in 45,000 refugees, almost half the number accepted in 2016.

You can play a part in helping our newest neighbors. Help refugees on their path to self-sufficiency by volunteering in ESL classes, youth programs, and citizenship classes. Donate household essentials or support the work of ReWA (rewa.org) or similar organizations financially. Also, make your voice heard. Contact your elected representatives (commoncause.org/find-your-representative/) and let them know that you support refugees and understand both their sacrifices and contributions.

INDEX

Misir Wot, 93
mitmita (spice blend)
    Kitfo, 92
Mixed Fried Rice, 105
Mohinga, 81–82
mozzarella cheese
    Warbat, 156–157
mushrooms
    Jiaozi, 19–21
    Mixed Fried Rice, 105
    Nga Baung Doke, 98–99
    Yao Hon, 55–57

N
Najwa (ReWA student)
    Lamb Kabsa, 101–103
Nan Gyi Thoke, 100
Nan-e Berenji, 149
Nan-e Nokhodchi, 150–151
napa cabbage
    Jiaozi, 19–21
    Yao Hon, 55–57
navy beans
    Cambuulo, 166
Nelson-Shimabukuro, Wadiyah, 167
Nga Baung Doke, 98–99
ngo gai (Vietnamese cilantro)
    Jinghpaw Shan Hkak, 126–127
Nguyen, Annie
    Chao Ga, 45
    journey, 44
Nguyen, Thoa
    journey, 22
    Saigon Chicken, Cabbage, and Mint Salad, 23–24
Nguyen, Thu-Van
    journey, 170–172
    Pho Ga, 65–67
Ni Ni (ReWA SeaTac student)
    journey, 79–80
    Mohinga, 81–82
    Nan Gyi Thoke, 100
Niter Kibbeh
    in Doro Wat, 62–63
    in Kitfo, 92
    recipe, 64
    in Shiro, 85

noodles
    Mohinga, 81–82
    Nan Gyi Thoke, 100
    Pho Ga, 65–67

O
okra
    Maraq, 83
    Sinigang, 76–78
Olivye, 34–35
onions. see also green onions; red onions; shallots
    Bariis, 49–50
    Chapli Kebab, 60–61
    Doro Wat, 62–63
    Fasolia, 27
    Goulash and Dumplings, 119
    Hilib Ari, 53
    Kebab, 114
    Kik Wot, 94
    Kitfo, 92
    Lamb Kabsa, 101–103
    Mantu, 89–90
    Misir Wot, 93
    Nga Baung Doke, 98–99
    Niter Kibbeh, 64
    Patacones con Hogao, 25–26
    Pho Ga, 65–67
    Poisson de Mer with Cassava and Pap, 69–70
    Pomegranate Khoresh with Chicken, 73–74
    Qabli, 116–117
    Shiro, 85
    Sinigang, 76–78
    Spiced Chicken, 48
    Vegetarian Borsch, 17–18
    Zereshk Polo Morgh, 87–88
    Zigni, 106
orange soda
    Basbousa, 138–139

P
palm sugar
    Chicken Satay, 2–3
    Yao Hon, 55–57
Pandan Extract
    in Banh Phuc Linh, 147–148
    in Kuih Seri Muka, 141–143

Pandan Extract (*cont.*)
    recipe, 144
pandan leaves
    Banh Phuc Linh, 147–148
    Pandan Extract, 144
Pap, 70
papayas
    Tum Bok Hoong, 28–29
parsley
    Maraq, 83
Patacones con Hogao, 25–26
peas
    Curry Puffs, 7–8
    Olivye, 34–35
peppers. see bell peppers; chilis
Persian cuisine. see Iran
Philippines
    Adobo, 107–109
    refugee journeys, 75
    Sinigang, 76–78
Pho Ga, 65–67
pickles
    Beet Salad Vinaigrette, 15
    Olivye, 34–35
pistachios
    Baklava, 154–155
    Warbat, 156–157
plantains
    Patacones con Hogao, 25–26
Poisson de Mer with Cassava and Pap, 69–70
Pomegranate Khoresh with Chicken, 73–74
pomegranate molasses (pomegranate paste)
    Pomegranate Khoresh with Chicken, 73–74
pomegranate seeds
    Pomegranate Khoresh with Chicken, 73–74
pompano
    Mohinga, 81–82
pork belly
    Adobo, 107–109
pork hocks
    Caldo Gallego, 120–122
    Sinigang, 76–78